THE
glorafilia
NEEDLEPOINT
COLLECTION

THE *glorafilia* NEEDLEPOINT COLLECTION

WITH COMPLETE PROJECTS AND STITCH CARDS

Jennifer Berman and Carole Lazarus

A DAVID & CHARLES CRAFT BOOK

To Sorel, Jason, Tamsin and Alison

British Library Cataloguing in Publication Data
Berman, Jennifer
The Glorafilia needlepoint collection: with complete
projects.
1. Canvas embroidery, – Manuals
I. Title II. Lazarus, Carole
746.442'2

ISBN 0–7153–9189–5

Typeset by Vine & Gorfin Ltd,
Exmouth, Devon
and printed in The Netherlands
by Royal Smeets Offset Weert
for David & Charles Publishers plc
Brunel House Newton Abbot Devon

Distributed in the United States by
Sterling Publishing Co Inc,
2, Park Avenue, New York, NY 10016

CONTENTS

INTRODUCTION

A visitor to our shop watched a canvas being worked and said, with some concern, 'All you're doing is filling in the holes with wool. Is that it?' Yes, that is it. In fact, that would make a good subtitle for this book: Glorafilia and the magical art of filling in holes with wool (or cotton, or silk, or ribbon, or metal thread . . .). Some elaboration is needed to explain the glorious fun this can be, an adventure in texture and colour and experimentation; the relaxing effect of placing one stitch after another to build a picture of richly interwoven threads. That's what needlepoint is. Some people call it tapestry, which is not correct; tapestries were woven and used to decorate and keep out draughts in baronial halls. 'Canvaswork embroidery' is a more accurate term for what this book is about, but those words conjure up a picture of a formal discipline with not too much spontaneity, and that's NOT what this book is about. Needlepoint can be compulsive fun; it can make hours spent in travel fly by, and it is the epitome of creative contentment to do by a fire in winter. It can even make you feel virtuous if you're not used to sitting doing 'nothing'. It is, in short, the delicious art of filling in holes with wool.

This book shows a variety of different themes and influences on our work, and also the way a canvas can be brought beautifully to life by using a variety of stitches – 'stitchery'. We explain why we have chosen to use the stitchery as we have, and how designs have been adapted from their source material, what effects we wanted, how that was achieved—and how you can do the same thing yourself. Each section has at least one design, sometimes more, to work from a chart or tracing. Our instructions are intended only as guides; do not be restricted by them, but use them as a stepping off point for your own creativity. We have kept to a minimum the chapter of general facts about needlepoint but we have included a complete set of unique Glorafilia stitch cards on which to learn and practise the stitches (see page 13). At the end of the book are instructions for making up the designs in various ways. We have covered themes in this book

that have excited us—including collaborating with the British Museum and the Royal Academy of Arts to produce needlepoint designs, re-establishing the traditional links between artist and craftsman. We have worked with interior designers, and on commissions which have developed into huge projects, and were beckoned down likely and unlikely routes. We have one foot rooted in the twentieth century and the other in the fifteenth, and dip, like butterflies, into many points between. And we realise more and more the magical antidote that needlepoint can be to the pressurised age in which we are living.

A needlepoint project can be a frivolity to be finished in a few hours, or an heirloom to be worked over many years—or, as with Henry James's poor heroine in *Washington Square*, 'Catherine, meanwhile, in the parlor, picking up her morsel of fancy

| *Right* A corner of the Glorafilia Shop

Antique accessories from the Glorafilia Shop

work, had seated herself with it again – for life, as it were.'

Glorafilia began 20 years ago—years of interwoven friendship, and a lot of water—in the form of coffee, champagne and tears—under a lot of bridges. We started it as a dried flower display company in the heady sixties, when people said, 'Dried flowers? Do you mean Dead Flowers?' The business continued until Jennifer moved to the United States and—considering we had been breaking new ground and flying in the face of convention—was surprisingly successful. The name Glorafilia sounded floral and, with one of those lovely coincidences that we insist on calling chance, the name (loosely interpreted) means Glorious Threads. What had we known about dried flowers, floral arrangements, window displays when we started Glorafilia I? Nothing. What did we know about needlepoint?

Knowing nothing about a subject is often a wonderful advantage—you can't be restricted by rules if you don't know what the rules are. It cuts out many of the limiting beliefs we hold about what we can do. That was in the beginning. Now, of course, we are restricted by a whole set of commercial considerations we never gave a thought to then—and it's a good thing that we are, otherwise we'd be enthusiastically producing unaffordable kits using pure silk, printed in 30 colours on canvas uncomfortably small to work and uncomfortably large to hold.

It would be nice to say here that the interest in

needlework had been with us both since childhood, but it wouldn't be quite true. However, that isn't to say there was no output at all. We are both sincerely convinced that at school we made needlecases for our mothers. We must have sewn on buttons here and there, hems when essential, the occasional nativity costume. We had both done one needlepoint cushion canvas and both abandoned them when it came to the boring background—the experience stood us in good stead and we determined, whenever possible, to have no 'background'. Not auspicious beginnings, but they show that almost anyone can do needlepoint!

Jennifer returned from America when the needlepointmania was running riot there (unfortunately we more restrained British are not given to such epidemics). A friend in New York, Harriett Sacks, had described an Italian scarf design she had wanted to make in needlepoint. 'I can do that,' said Jennifer, and painted the first Glorafilia canvas. The stitched cushion has gone into our 'memorabilia' pile and Harriett now runs Glorafilia in the US.

We looked in the stores for kits that we would like to have in our own homes and found nothing. The idea began to grow. We gathered canvas, wools, needles, painted a few designs, which were snapped up by friends and, from the same enthusiasm and disregard for convention as its predecessor, Glorafilia II was born. Pregnancies have played an important part in Glorafilia's creativity. Our original collection of designs, some of which are still in our range, was created with Carole confined to bed for six months—we spent the time devising colourways, stitches and themes, perched together on an eighteenth-century French bed, both fascinated by the effects coming from our needles as we transformed anonymous canvas and yarn into pieces of richly textured fabric. During Jennifer's last pregnancy, when she needed a long, involved project to get her teeth into, she devised Learn Needlepoint, the complete course in a kit.

Our collection of kits ready, nobody wanted to buy them. Needlework shops were committed to traditional ideas and we ran into the Catch 22 of their wanting only to buy roses, because that's all their customers would buy, because that was all they stocked, etc. Then Liberty (of London) and Tricia Guild (of Designers Guild) asked us to work with their fabrics; that broke the chain and enabled us to lift needlepoint out of the haberdashery department and into interior decoration, where it belonged.

We came to needlepoint from different experiences—interior decorating and portrait painting—both of which, at that time, were too demanding to fit into the greater demands of families. How we have changed! Glorafilia has slowly overtaken us in an all-encompassing way and we are fiercely protective of it, even though it swings between angelic and enfant terrible phases. Jennifer is never without clipboard and stocklists and, at catalogue time, Carole is like a New York Bag Lady, carrying copy, layouts, transparencies everywhere in case the car is stolen/the house catches fire/the office is ransacked, until the whole package is handed over to the printer—and we are probably also the only clients who stand by the presses to check every print run for colour accuracy. When we began to mass produce our kits, it was this same determination for excellence that made us continue to handpaint the designs until we found Fred in Devon, the only printer it seemed who would work to the standard we wanted. Oh, why isn't the world full of Freds? One time, in a dock strike, with no Swiss canvas in this country, Jennifer drove to Switzerland to collect rolls of it,

Above Glorafilia is in an eighteenth-century mill house in London's charming Mill Hill Village, like a surprising Aladdin's cave amid fields and duckponds, trotting horses and breathtaking views

Below Jennifer's sitting room, with its 'country house' atmosphere and pastel colouring, perfect for showing off these needlepoint cushions

9

Carole and Jennifer photographed in Carole's house – a unique photograph, such tranquillity is unusual!

rather than compromise on the quality. Obsessive? Fanatical? Absolutely!

Our children grew up in a world where Jason believed that 'a Mummy is someone who paints canvases' and Tamsin knew that 'eggs come from chickens, milk comes from cows, wool comes from the garage'. Jason and Sorel know, if they can remember that far back, that there was a life before Glorafilia. For Tamsin and Alison (who was almost born in the shop) life has always had Glorafilia at its core. We worked from our respective homes, which began to look more and more like the inside of mills—rainbows of wool on door handles, chair-backs, banisters; a journey across a room was like negotiating a minefield of canvas and paint. Our families were, mostly, magnificently tolerant. There were bulk canvas-cutting sessions, painters delivering canvases, canvas edges being taped by hand until we discovered the right machine, wool being plaited, kits being rolled and ribboned. People developed what we still call the 'Glorafilia Walk', long spidery steps, as if on eggshells, to avoid drying canvases.

Finally, we burst out of our homes and into the Old Mill House, launching it with our first ambitious catalogue and consolidating the team who are still with us today. With the Old Mill House came the shop, which gives us a showcase and an excellent opportunity for feedback from customers. It sits, like a tiny Aladdin's cave, in the original heart of Mill Hill, one of London's most picturesque old villages. The most horrendous

winter followed our move to the Old Mill House, with deep snow drifts that prevented all but two members of staff getting to the shop. There were no customers; the postman somehow made it up the hill, but disaster did not result—far from it—the mail order business boomed and that was, perhaps, the real start of Glorafilia as it is today.

From those early days of painting all canvases by hand, most of our designs are now printed, and we Londoners love to visit the Lancashire mill which produces most of them. It is in a tiny street and the mill is like something from an abandoned sepia photograph. We resist looking through the school windows in case the pupils are not wearing pinafores and don't have their books tied in a strap. The moors behind are always painted November, and the street is grey, brown, just-rained-on beige. We feel like intruders from another age whenever we visit, but importantly, our work being produced there now gives sense and continuity to a craft that has always spoken volumes about the age it represents.

There is a certain attitude to needlework that we hope is lessening. We call it the 'Don't Look At the Back' syndrome, and imagine it must have been handed on from school, the strait-laced approach to sewing and getting it 'right'. But what is right? You will be instructed in the correct way to do your needlepoint by many sources and all will be different and all perpetuate a rigid discipline that inhibits creativity. Somewhere along the way the word 'enjoyment' is often forgotten. There is no question that, as with any skill, it is necessary to master the basics—in this case a few stitches—in order to work freely and effortlessly. And for many of us the journey is as important as the arrival. We don't hand out reprimands to customers with untidy 'backs' (though by their embarrassment they seem to expect it). Instead we ask, 'Did you enjoy doing it?' and they always say, 'Oh, yes!' One of our favourite customers zaps through cushions at an extraordinary speed; the fronts look fine, the backs like a dish of spaghetti, and they exude all the enthusiasm we're sure she brings to all she does. We stretch them for her and make them up; they look great, and then they are probably thrown onto a chair and never noticed again. A traveller rather than an arriver.

Whether working in stitchery, or designing your own canvas, there should be an element of play. Look at a painting by a child—not a thought for, 'Shall I? shan't I?'—the spontaneity of doing it is all

that matters. Somehow we must find that little child inside ourselves again, to jump in with both feet, and just delight in what we can do.

And the secret of a partnership that is still creative after fourteen years? We are both different in every way; we disagree horribly and love each other greatly. We can still laugh like schoolchildren over the same things, because our shared experiences cover a lot of time. Our tastes are quite different; our homes are poles apart in appearance—one is light, floral and festooned with lace and frills, the other sombre and theatrical with rich dramatic colours. Somewhere in the middle we dance around a compromise that seems to work.

Our greatest pleasure (apart from locking the office door for ten days at Christmas) lies in people all over the world who enjoy working our designs, in whatever city, mountain or desert they may be. It's a wonderful thought, and still gratifies and amazes us.

GENERAL
INFORMATION

DESIGNS

This book is divided into themes, and for each we have given a project, or projects. These are varied and include cushions, pictures, photoframes, a rug; some are very simple, some ambitious. Each describes how the design developed and why the stitches used were chosen, as well as how to achieve the same result. The explanation will show the route we take in creating a piece and hopefully will convey that there is no mystery about any of it!

Each project will explain how to mark out the canvas, what stitches are used, how to make up the project into a cushion, photoframe, spectacle case, etc, and what materials you will need. All you need to stitch each individual project: needles, canvas cut to size, and relevant yarn can be obtained from Glorafilia (see back flap of jacket).

STITCHES

The stitch cards and diagrams will help you master the different stitches we use throughout the book.

They are an excellent way to learn, whether you do most of them, for a project like Learn Needlepoint, or whether you just pick out those you need for the design you have chosen. Once stitched they can be kept for reference.

Turn to the back flap of the jacket for information on how to obtain your folder containing 25 stitch cards—absolutely free of charge.

YARNS

We use four yarns mainly: tapestry wool, crewel wool, coton perlé and stranded cotton. Tapestry wool is the most widely used for 14 canvas as it covers perfectly. It comes in an enormous number of glorious colours. Crewel wool is very fine wool; three strands of it are equivalent to one of tapestry wool. It is wonderfully versatile, with the advantage that the shades can be mixed to give gradations of colour and subtleties not possible with tapestry wool. Being finer, it can be used on smaller gauge canvas for more detailed designs or several strands can be put together to sew a larger gauge canvas. The shading of the 'Morning, Volterra' figure page 102 and the borders of the 'Pierrot' and 'Columbine' page 106 were achieved with crewel wool. It was also used for the Monet chair, which was worked on 7-gauge canvas using five strands, and on the 'Monet Poppies' using one or two strands to achieve the fine flow of the stitches.

Coton perlé comes in two thicknesses, No 3, suitable for 14 canvas and No 5, for 18 canvas; it has a twist in it which reflects light and gives a beautifully lustrous effect. Stranded cotton, also called embroidery silk, has the sheen of coton perlé, but because it has no twist, it has the satisfying density of wool. We like using this yarn more and more—because it is stranded it also has the versatility of crewel. In addition, we use metal thread and 4-ply rug wool.

CANVAS

We always use single thread (mono) canvas, simply because it's the most pleasant to use, interlocked for printed designs and deluxe for those charted and handpainted designs that need to follow precisely the thread of the canvas.

On printed or handpainted designs we use white canvas as it shows the colours clearly, particularly in artificial light. However, when the designs are not painted on the canvas and the yarn colours are dark, white canvas may show through. In this case antique canvas may be a better choice. Alternatively, a white canvas can be primed with a wash of thin oil-paint in an appropriate colour. Leave it to dry thoroughly before stitching.

The edges of the canvas should be taped with masking tape before you begin to sew, to prevent canvas, yarn and tempers fraying.

MARKING OUT THE CANVAS

It is important to note that, when drawing lines on your canvas, you follow the thread of the canvas unless told to do otherwise (Figs 1 and 2). It is especially important that when diagonal lines are drawn you follow either the 'under' or 'over' threads of the canvas.

For CHAIN stitch you follow the groove between the threads of the canvas. Diagonally follow both the 'under' and 'over' threads (Fig 3).

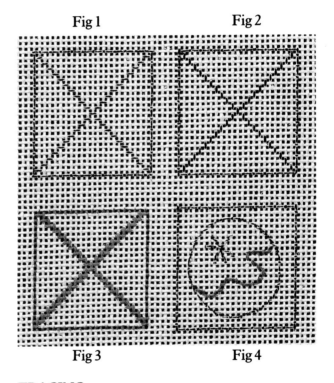

Fig 1   Fig 2

Fig 3   Fig 4

TRACING

All tracings appear on pages 168–89. When tracing a design, follow the curved lines freely, regardless of the canvas grid. A second colour can be used to differentiate between the shades of wool (Fig 4). When tracing straight lines, use your discretion by marking the outline on the closest thread.

WORKING FROM COLOUR CHARTS

When working from colour charts, remember that each square represents the intersection of the canvas and not the hole between the thread. When using

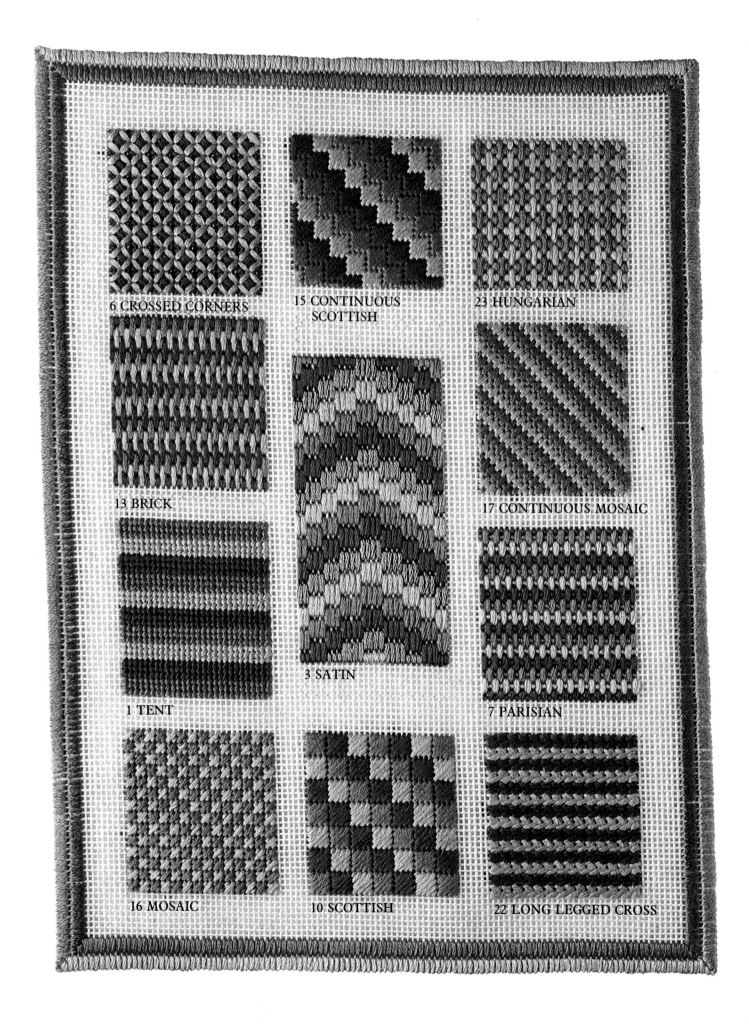

6 CROSSED CORNERS

15 CONTINUOUS
SCOTTISH

23 HUNGARIAN

13 BRICK

17 CONTINUOUS MOSAIC

1 TENT

3 SATIN

7 PARISIAN

16 MOSAIC

10 SCOTTISH

22 LONG LEGGED CROSS

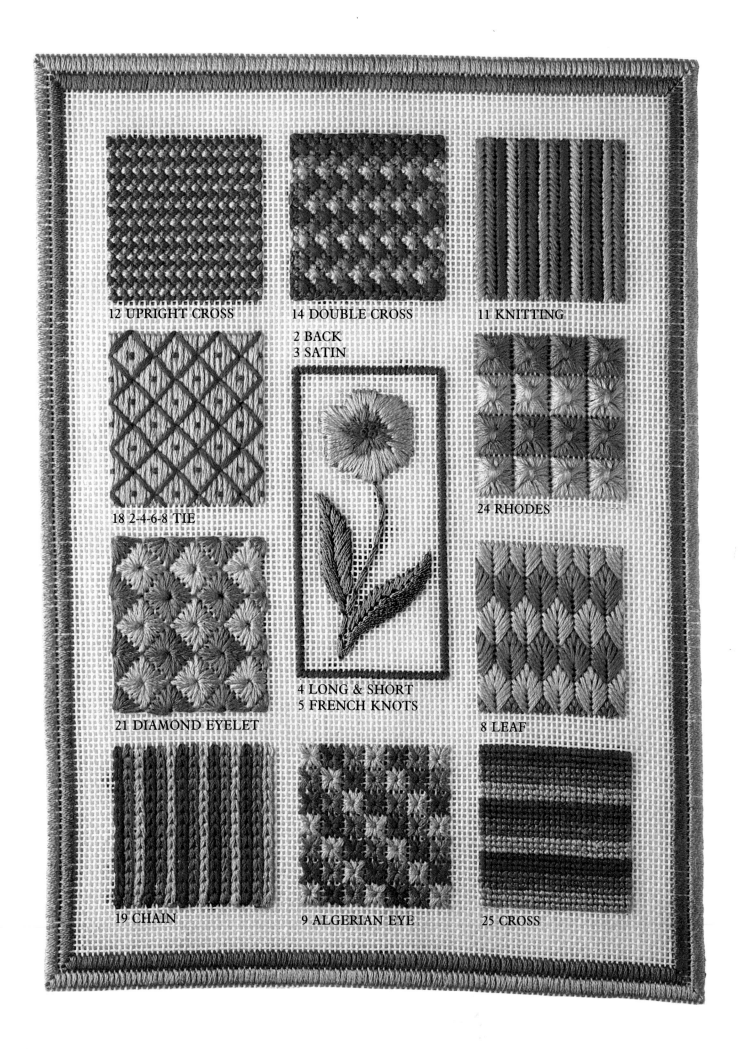

12 UPRIGHT CROSS

14 DOUBLE CROSS

11 KNITTING

2 BACK
3 SATIN

18 2-4-6-8 TIE

24 RHODES

21 DIAMOND EYELET

4 LONG & SHORT
5 FRENCH KNOTS

8 LEAF

19 CHAIN

9 ALGERIAN EYE

25 CROSS

CANVAS/YARN/NEEDLE CHART

Single thread canvas (mono)	Appleton's tapestry wool in skeins or 25gr hanks* Anchor tapisserie in skeins	Appleton's crewel wool in skeins or 25gr hanks	DMC coton perlé Nos 3 & 5 in skeins	Anchor stranded cotton in skeins (6 strands per thread)	Size of tapestry needle
10 holes to the inch (4 per cm)		4/5 threads depending on size of stitch		9/12 strands	18
14 holes to the inch (5 per cm)	1 thread	3 threads	No 3 1 thread	6/9 strands	20
16 holes to the inch (6 per cm)		2/3 threads depending on size of stitch	No 5 1–2 threads No 3 1 thread	6 strands	22
18 holes to the inch (7 per cm)		2 threads	No 5 1 thread	4/6 strands	22

*The formula is that two 30in (75cm) lengths of tapestry wool will cover one square inch in tent stitch. Therefore one 25gr hank (72×30in lengths) will cover approximately 36 sq inches.

tent stitch or cross stitch each square represents one stitch (Fig 5), but sometimes several squares represent one stitch if stitchery is used (ie 'Victorian Circle' project in Chapter 9).

Before beginning to stitch it is advisable to mark the top of the canvas, so that if you turn the canvas while stitching you will know where the top is.

The graph paper we have used has units of 10 squares × 10 squares to make stitching easier. Mark out your canvas with a permanent marker, in a suitable colour, in units of 10 × 10 squares.

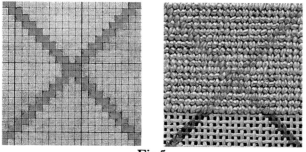

Fig 5

FRAMES

Using a frame is a personal choice. If you use a frame the method of working is different—the needle is passed front to back, back to front, etc, with a stabbing motion, rather than completing the stitch in one 'sewing' movement. There is no question that you will get a straighter finish and more even tension if you use a frame. However, if you prefer to do your needlepoint curled up in a chair with the work rolled up in your hand, that's fine too! Just one point, if you don't use a frame try not to pull the canvas too tightly as this will distort it; and roll the unworked part up to the point you're working rather than crushing it. This applies particularly when using cotton, as a lot of handling removes the sheen.

There are two basic types of frame—the most popular is the rotating lap frame which comes in different widths, and can be used in any way you find comfortable, supported against a table, chair, arms or knees; it is portable, or there is a floor

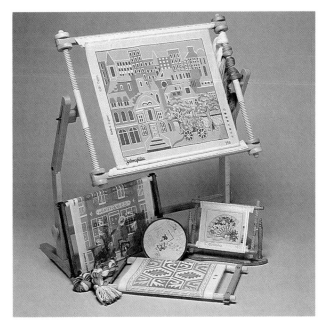

standing frame, which is ideal as it leaves both hands free.

OTHER MATERIALS YOU MAY NEED

Large scissors, for cutting canvas. Small pointed embroidery scissors. A thimble, not necessary, just personal preference. Masking tape to bind the edges of the canvas. Permanent markers, HB pencil, Pikaby's Water Erasable Marking Pen for marking canvas. (Whatever is used must be either waterproof or water erasable, so that when the canvas is damped and stretched nothing 'bleeds'.) Ruler, tape measure. Eraser. Compass.

If you ever need to unpick expanses of work an unpicker (made by Pikaby) is very useful—there are few things, root-canal work included, as little fun as unpicking tent on 18 canvas!

SOME NEEDLEPOINT FACTS

It is important to sit in a good light.

Leave approximately 2in (5cm) of border around the edge of the worked canvas in order to stretch the canvas into shape after sewing (see stretching instructions at the end of the book).

Before you begin stitching, cut your wool to approximately 30in (75cm), cotton and crewel wool to 15in to 20in (38 to 51cm).

Where to begin? There are no rules. We work outlining first so that it recedes a little as the other stitches are worked. In general, leave the background until the rest is done and then just 'fill-in' around the image.

Try and leave white yarn to the end, if possible, to keep it clean, and avoid catching loose ends of other colours into the stitches.

When working with stitchery you will find that there are times when there are insufficient canvas threads to complete a stitch, and where this applies use 'compensating' stitches, small filling-in stitches (see stitch cards).

If you are preparing to do tent stitch on a large area, try using basketweave. The effect on the front is the same, but it puts no strain on the canvas and a less 'linear' finish results.

HOW TO THREAD A NEEDLE!

The best way is to fold the yarn firmly over the thinnest part of the needle, pinch it tightly between thumb and forefinger, as close as possible to the needle, remove the needle and push the eye of the needle over the folded yarn and ease through. Much easier than it sounds—try it!

HOW TO START AND FINISH

To begin: knot the wool temporarily on the front of the canvas about 1in (2.5cm) from where you want to start *in the direction in which you will be working.* As you work your canvas, the stitches on the back will anchor the 1in (2.5cm) thread. When you reach the knot, cut it off and the thread should be quite secure. When you re-thread your needle to continue the same area, there is no need to knot the wool, simply run the needle through the work on the underside. And to finish do the same in reverse.

KEEP THE BACK TIDY

There are two simple reasons why it helps. First, having the back like a crow's nest can eventually make it difficult to get your needle through. Secondly, the work will lie flatter when it's made up. Not vital, but quite logical.

AND FINALLY . . .

When framing, we never use glass. Nor would we put glass on an oil painting. These are tactile, textured pieces and deserve to be enjoyed as such, not flattened and diminished behind glass. Just flick over with a feather duster and, since needlepoint is a good way of smoking less, ideally they should not be in a smoky atmosphere.

Cushions can be Scotch Guarded, and despite what Our Shirlee will tell you, we strongly recommend that you do *not* wash your needlepoint. Take it to a good dry cleaner.

CHAPTER 1
TOWN SCENE AND GEOMETRIC STITCHERY

The 'Town Scene' first really woke us up to stitchery. It was a design always somewhere in the back of the mind; childhood images of toytown houses on a hillside, seemingly standing on top of each other; illustrations from Babar the Elephant, from Positano, medieval walled towns or, nearer to home, the view of Bath as you approach by train. Something fascinating about the jigsaw shapes that from a distance appear two-dimensional. There have been New York scenes, Victorian scenes since this was done, but 'Town Scene' has always been our favourite. We experienced for the first time the fascinating way the juxtaposed stitches took over the design and for that reason this is the most significant of all Glorafilia designs.

We were already charmed by the possibilities that stitchery presented, and the choice of turning a flat picture into a strongly textured semi-abstract sampler. 'Town Scene' had wonderful potential for just that and through stitchery we were able to communicate the rough and smooth, the soft and concrete qualities the design dictated. We experimented, and saw the nature of the colours alter depending on how they were worked and positioned. We enjoyed the fact that portrayal of bricks need not just give the impression of bricks, they

The Town Scene, the design that made us realise the possibilities of stitchery. It was the first time the individual stitches took over the design, creating fascinating dimensions

could actually *be* bricks (albeit wool bricks), so many tactile illusions, receding, leaping out; it was an enchanting new dimension, with each stitch either harmoniously complementing, or aggressively arguing with its neighbour. Either way exciting the eye—a new, surprising world. The passion for stitchery was established.

The design for this section is a miniature scene of Jerusalem, worked in beautiful, jewel colours. Like 'Town Scene', a balance has been achieved through the choice of stitchery, using tent stitch as an 'antidote'. Overall complex stitches would be confusing but, by containing the areas, with receding tent stitch windows and a flat tent stitch sky to provide an essential contrast, visual indigestion is avoided.

From 'Town Scene' came the geometrics and satisfying mathematical designs. Still a far cry from free interpretation but a challenging use of the grid system of the canvas. The geometric designs are still handpainted—it is impossible to print a complicated geometric canvas with total accuracy as the canvas might not be absolutely square. For this reason we shall always have handpainted designs in our range. We both spent a long time painting geometrics and were not displeased when tastes eventually became softer.

At Glorafilia we all have favourite different stitches and we can tell which of our team has worked something, simply because of the bias towards particular stitchery. Continuous mosaic is a delightful stitch, like little interlocking zips, very textural, whereas Parisian, which is the same stitch

upright, always seems dull. Somebody else could feel the opposite. The brown and terracotta geometric cushion is a marvellous combination of quite simple stitch techniques, put together with boldness and balance.

'Eastward and Westward Ducks' show the way stitchery can change a design. From simple pictures, this pair of cushions have become multi-layer textural pieces, with the stitchery working as impasto paint would work—but not by building up artificially—simply by changing stitch.

'Mothers and Her Daughters', too, is an example of stitchery working in its own right and creating extra dimensions. Using repeated stitches, movement and flow is suggested simply and successfully. This shows that it is possible to take a simply-drawn theme and allow the stiches to make it rich and vibrant.

Above Mother and Her Daughters, an excellent example of stitchery making the design

Left The Eastward and Westward Ducks

Right Some geometric designs – the Lotus design cushion on the chair has been enlarged to make the carpet canvas shown

JERUSALEM

Finished size of design: 11½ × 10in (29 × 26cm)
Tracing: page 171

MATERIALS
Appleton's crewel wool

GR	Green	436	3 skeins
O	Ochre	696	3 skeins
M	Maroon	505	2 skeins
C	Crimson	995	1 skein
R	Royal	464	2 skeins
N	Navy	747	6 skeins
B	Black	993	1 skein
P	Purple	456	1 skein

DMC coton perlé No 5

E	Emerald	943	1 skein
Y	Yellow	744	1 skein
G	Gold	783	2 skeins

Antique mono deluxe canvas, 18 holes to the inch
Canvas size: 16 × 15in (41 × 38cm)
Size 22 needle
Ruler or tape measure

Masking tape for binding the canvas
Sharp scissors for cutting the canvas
Embroidery scissors
Sharp HB pencil or fine permanent marker in a
  suitable colour
Eraser

HOW TO MARK THE CANVAS
Cut the canvas to size and tape the edges. Place the drawing (page 171) centrally under the canvas and trace the design. Vertical and horizontal lines should be on the thread of the canvas. Draw a line around it.

HOW TO STITCH
Coton perlé is used for the yellow on the dome, the gold areas and the emerald areas—the whole thread has been used. Crewel wool has been used everywhere else—three strands have been used for all horizontal and vertical stitches. Two strands have been used for all diagonal stitches and tent stitch.

Stitches used
1   tent stitch
2   back stitch
3   satin stitch
7   Parisian stitch
9   Algerian eye stitch
12 upright cross stitch

13   brick stitch
16   mosaic stitch
17   continuous mosaic stitch

The stitch cards will show you how to do the stitches. The numbers on the diagram refer to the numbers on the stitch cards. Where there is no number, TENT stitch has been used. The letters refer to the colours. The areas filled in with black are worked in black wool.

The black arrows show the direction of the stitches. The red arrows are to point out the colours and stitch numbers. *Where there is an asterisk, SATIN stitch is worked in rows over three threads.

BRICK stitch is worked horizontally or vertically over four threads and also over two threads. Refer to the colour picture—large areas are over four threads; small areas over two threads.

Work from the top right hand corner and leave the coton perlé to the end. If coton perlé is handled too much, it will lose its lustre.

If you want to use other stitches please feel free to do so. This is a guide—do not be restricted by it.

MAKING UP INSTRUCTIONS
After the design has been sewn it may be necessary to stretch it back to shape and then you can frame it or make it into a cushion (Chapter 15). If you decide to frame it, we suggest you take it to a professional framer, who will also stretch it for you.

CHECKERBOARD

Size: 13½in square (34cm)
Colours: Marine Blue
              Rose Pink
Tracing: page 168

MATERIALS

1A MARINE BLUE
Appleton's tapestry wool
P   Pale Blue   321   1¼ hanks (90 × 30in/75cm lengths)
D   Dark Blue   323   1¼ hanks (90 × 30in/75cm lengths)
W   White   991   ½ hank (36 × 30in/75cm lengths)
DMC coton perlé No 3
B   Bright Blue 322   6 skeins

1B ROSE PINK
Appleton's tapestry wool
P   Pale Pink   141   1¼ hanks (90 × 30in/75cm lengths)
D   Dark Pink   143   1¼ hanks (90 × 30in/75cm lengths)
W   White   991   ½ hank (36 × 30in/75cm lengths)
DMC coton perlé No 3
B   Bright Pink 3687 6 skeins

Antique mono deluxe canvas or white with a wash of   colour on it, 14 holes to the inch
Canvas size = 17½in square (44cm)

Right Checkerboard design, shown in two colourways

Size 20 needle
Ruler or tape measure
Masking tape for binding the canvas
Sharp scissors for cutting the canvas
Embroidery scissors
Sharp HB pencil or fine permanent marker in a suitable
  colour
Eraser

HOW TO MARK THE CANVAS
Cut the canvas to size and tape the edges.

Diagram 1 Starting about 2in (5cm) diagonally in from the top righthand corner (A) draw a horizontal line approximately 13½in (34cm) long following the thread of the canvas. From the top righthand corner (A) draw a vertical line approximately 13½in (34cm) long.

From A count down 38 holes and draw a horizontal line following the thread of the canvas. Repeat this until there are 6 horizontal lines approximately 13½in (34cm) long. Then do the same vertically so that there are 5 squares on each side, 25 squares in all.

Trace the gardenia motif (page 168) onto the canvas in the bottom righthand corner of the design leaving 1in (2.5cm) from the edge of the design.

Diagram 2 Finally form the diamonds (except under the gardenia) by counting 12 holes from the cross and drawing 4 diagonal lines to meet on the 'over' or 'under' thread of the canvas. Repeat until all the diamonds are formed with half diamonds on the sides. You will now have formed hexagonals and diamonds. Ignore or erase the cross in the middle of the diamonds. Your marked-out canvas should look like Diagram 3.

HOW TO STITCH
The whole thread is used throughout.

Stitches used
  1 tent stitch
  2 back stitch
  3 satin stitch
  5 French knots
13 brick stitch

The stitch cards will show you how to do the stitches. Refer to Diagram 3 for the position and direction of the stitches. The fine lines and the arrows refer to the direction. The letters refer to the colours and the numbers refer to the stitch card numbers.

Outline the hexagonal and diamond shapes with coton perlé in TENT stitch (B1) reversing the direction of the stitch on two sides of the diamonds—see arrows. The gardenia and leaves are also outlined in coton perlé in BACK stitch (B2). The hexagonal shapes are filled in with two shades of wool in BRICK stitch over four threads, the pale shade in vertical BRICK stitch (P13), the dark shade in horizontal BRICK stitch (D13). The diamonds are worked in coton perlé in TENT stitch (B1). The leaves on the gardenia are in two shades of wool in SATIN stitch (P3 and D3) and the gardenia is sewn in white SATIN stitch (W3) radiating out from the centre. The middle of the flower is worked in FRENCH KNOTS (W5). Finally sew a line of TENT stitch in coton perlé around the design (B1).

The effect is simple but dramatic. This is an easy design to adapt to different sizes, perfect for chair seats or a stool. Experiment with this design using different and more complicated stitches. The design is perfect for a beginner.

MAKING UP INSTRUCTIONS
After you have finished stitching the design, stretch back into shape and then make into a cushion (see Chapter 15).

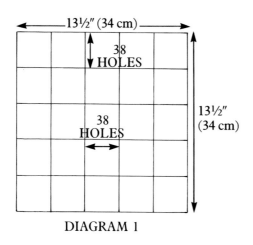

DIAGRAM 1

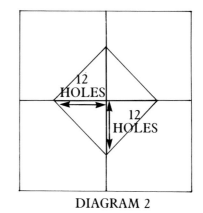

DIAGRAM 2

DIAGRAM 3

CHAPTER 2
BAMBOO
AND
TRELLIS

In the 1950s, many homes had only just begun to recover from the war, and the great spending boom of later years on consumer products and the 'dressing' of the home had not yet begun. Young couples setting up home had scant choice for their furnishings and little exposure to design. By the 1960s, as with other trends and feelings, a new breeze was blowing and attention was turning to style and fashion in clothes and furnishing.

In dress it was 'freedom and flower power'; in furnishing the word of the day was Scandinavian. Even in the High Street, taste was gradually being changed with the introduction of stores that offered reasonably priced 'designed' furniture and accessories, within the price range of most consumers. The stark simple lines coming from Sweden and Denmark left no room for the traditional style tapestry designs of previous years.

By the late sixties and early seventies, a different look began to emerge—a departure from functional furniture towards influences of the East, with people once more travelling to the orient and adopting its ideas and tastes. There were perhaps other factors, a resurgence of nostalgia, for Edwardian rattan ware and leisured images; a new emphasis on outdoor living, lighter colours, lighter atmosphere, conservatories bringing the outside inside.

Bamboo and cane have had a recurring decorative cycle since the eighteenth century—think of Chinese Chippendale and also the influence of Regency furniture. The seventies upsurge of enthusiasm for bamboo and cane meant that it was everywhere—on bedheads, mirror frames, pens, carpets, walls—painted on furniture, printed on textiles.

For us, bamboo, cane and trellis were a joy and have become a theme we use repeatedly in needlework (see overleaf). Their shapes marry perfectly with the natural dictates of the canvas. It can be rustic or sophisticated. It is harmonious with flowers and foliage, which we love to use. Trellis is a device which creates background depth simply, without interfering with the subject.

Interwoven trellis was one of the ways we first experimented with stitchery, the satisfying interlocking of satin stitches over and under, as seen in the 'Fuchsia and Cane' cushion on page 36.

Two of the first bamboo designs we did were 'Butterfly Bamboo' and 'Shell Bamboo' (right). The colours are quite chameleon—the green is in fact an elephant grey and the background appears a neutral beige but is in fact peach, so the design blends wonderfully almost anywhere. We have strongly mixed memories of these cushions. We designed them for an early magazine offer. Unfortunately, the publication was hit by a printing strike and cancelled, leaving us knee deep in wool, canvases, instructions, etc. On Christmas Eve we were told that the issue would appear after all, so we spent Christmas and the New Year taping canvases, plaiting wool, packing kits, with our husbands in less than glowing Yuletide good humour. We realised too late the benefits of the extended family (created for just such an emergency) and had to resort to child sweat-shop labour.

We use cane and trellis on cushions, around wall hangings, on large designs like carpets and tiny designs like pincushions—on anything and everything! Because of the canvas grid the diamond becomes a pleasing and easy shape, and by simply following the weave delightful patterns can be made to flow naturally one after another, adapting beautifully to stark modern lines, classic French looks or oriental intricacies. With the hint of a shadowed edge, a three dimensional look can be suggested, and with just fine lines it is possible to create an effective depth of background.

BUTTERFLY TRELLIS

Finished size of design: 10in × 8½in (25 × 22cm)
Tracing: page 169

MATERIALS
DMC coton perlé No 3

Peach	754	1 skein
Salmon	758	1 skein
Orange	402	1 skein
Grey	414	1 skein
Elephant	642	1 skein
Beige	842	3 skeins
Sand	738	1 skein
Ginger	437	1 skein
White	Blanc	5 skeins

White interlocked canvas, 14 holes to the inch
Canvas size: 14in × 13in (36 × 33cm)
Size 20 needle
Ruler or tape measure
Masking tape for binding the canvas
Sharp scissors for cutting the canvas
Embroidery scissors
Sharp HB pencil or fine permanent marker
Eraser

HOW TO MARK THE CANVAS
Cut the canvas to size and tape the edges. Trace the butterfly (page 169) centrally onto the canvas.

HOW TO STITCH
Use the whole thread throughout.

STITCHES USED
 1 tent stitch
 2 split back stitch
 3 satin stitch
17 continuous mosaic stitch
19 chain stitch

The stitch cards will show you how to do the stitches The numbers on the drawing refer to the numbers on the stitch cards. Refer to the colour picture and to the colour chart (overleaf) to show you which colour goes where and the direction of the stitches—the arrows show the direction.

Stitch the butterfly beginning with the body in CONTINUOUS MOSAIC stitch (17) and then the wings in SATIN stitch (3). Break the stitch on the dotted lines where marked on the tracing. Some outlining and the antennae are in SPLIT BACK stitch (2). The black areas on the tracing are to be sewn in CHAIN stitch (19).

The background has been worked in vertical SATIN stitch (3) in a diamond trellis pattern in beige 842 and TENT stitch (1) in blanc (white). In order to work the design so that you finish at the edge of a diamond, begin to stitch where indicated on the colour chart. Count the squares from the top of the butterfly's body (between the antennae). SATIN stitch (3) has been worked over three threads. Note the change of pattern where the trellis crosses. When you have finished sewing the trellis, work the background in white TENT stitch (1).

There should be 9 complete diamonds and 2 half diamonds along the top and 10 complete diamonds along the bottom; 8½ diamonds along the sides.

Finally sew a line of TENT stitch (1) around the edge of the design.

This is a perfect design to enlarge or adapt. Enlarge butterfly drawings from a book and trace them in different positions. The trellis can be extended—it would make a beautiful chair seat or stool.

MAKING UP INSTRUCTIONS
After you have finished stitching, the design may need to be stretched back into shape then made up into a cushion (see Chapter 15) or take it to a framer if you would like it framed.

Right The Butterfly Trellis cushion

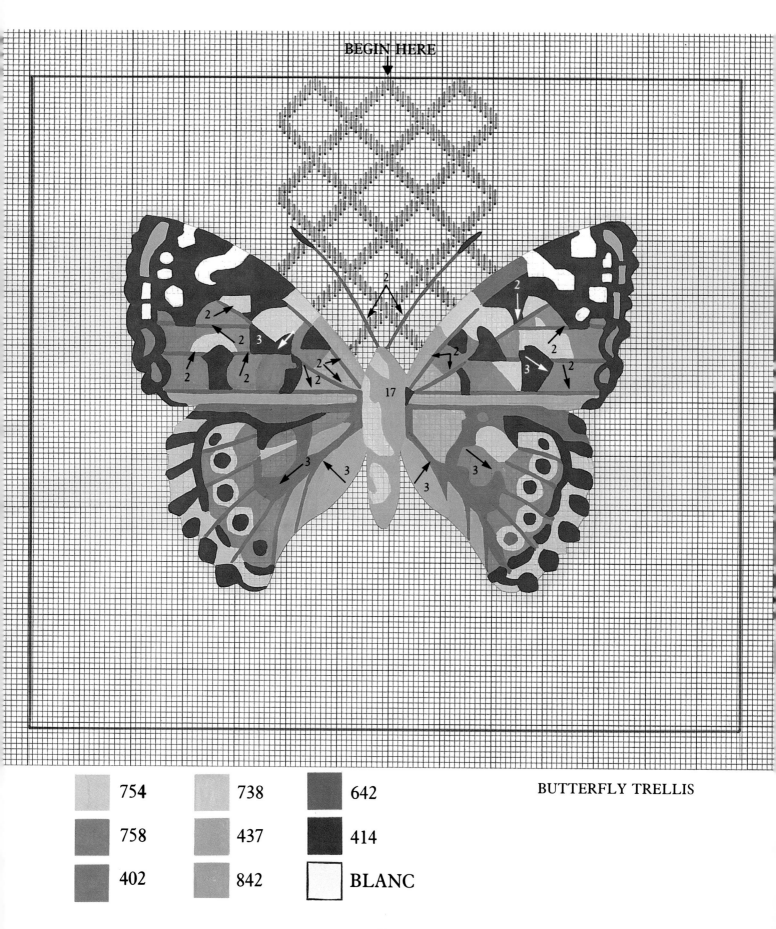

BEGIN HERE

BUTTERFLY TRELLIS

754
758
402
738
437
842
642
414
BLANC

CHAPTER 3
ADAPTATIONS

The first time our needlepoint kits were accepted commercially was when we adapted textile designs for Liberty and Designers Guild. The distinct personality of their fabrics was a joy to work with. We had long been fascinated by the art of assembling collages, juxtaposing images to create something fresh, and over the years we had made many for friends and family. It looks deceptively simple to arrange (and rearrange) photographs, memorabilia, a love letter, an invitation, fabric, into a personal and pleasing picture—this was just translating those principles into another medium.

To adapt a furnishing fabric into needlepoint, first pick out the colours and motifs you want to use—everyone will interpret the same piece of fabric differently. With either colour or shape, you are starting from a definite reference point and after that you can improvise at will. Cut up the material, trace shapes from it, arrange them, reduce or

Below Some of our collages

Overleaf Some of the designs adapted from fabric, including Liberty's Briar Rose (top, left), Colefax & Fowler's Fuchsias and Designers Guild Paper Roses

enlarge them, repeat them. If you are not happy sketching, use a photocopier. And if you are not pleased with these initial ideas, start again. Since this is *your* cushion, you make the rules! If you are not certain if the design balances, look at it in a mirror and any oddities will leap out. Realising that your work is unique to you will not only give you great pleasure, but confidence to do more. The best designs are those that fall into place easily. If nothing breaks the harmony, if your eye travels happily over the image and colouring without coming to a sharp stop, if it pleases you, then you have the ingredients for success. A design that needs to be altered, rearranged greatly between concept and conclusion and still seems awkward, should be scrapped. Yarn colours should be compatible when held in a bunch—though keep in mind that proportion of colour will not be accurate. There is the added element that stitchery changes colour value according to the size of the stitch— longer stitches are lighter and small stitches, like tent, because of all the busy shadows, appear darker. So, experiment. Work little pieces of canvas, try different stitchery. If it doesn't look right unpick it. And unpick it again, if necessary. If the basic concept is sound, but you're still unsure, come back to it—sometimes in isolation colours will not work, but when the neighbouring pieces are worked, all will blend quite happily.

The designs in this chapter have all taken fabric, or china, as their inspiration. The Liberty designs (on page 36) both have Glorafilia input: the geometric borders, the striped background, con-

taining the 'fabric' in a diamond shape. 'Briar Rose' must be one of their most famous designs, but the use of the fabric direct, however beautiful, would miss the opportunity for additional dimensions. And without those additions and the stitchery, a cushion may as well be made up in the fabric itself.

The Designers Guild designs show stylised florals which were a delight to work with. Today, so many fabrics come co-ordinated that you can 'jigsaw' them around (see the 'Inverwoven Ribbon' cushion in this section). The reasoning behind the 'ribbons' is that the pattern is narrow and the overlapping device is one we enjoy using—it keeps design elements separate and yet together. Another way of treating these co-ordinating designs would have been to use a border, or borders within borders.

In the Colefax & Fowler 'Tree Poppies' it seemed to us that the key to the design is the brush strokes on the flowers. The lines printed on the petals have been echoed perfectly in the long and short stitch, thus keeping the 'personality' of the fabric.

The beautiful Copeland Spode china that makes Jennifer's kitchen glow like a jewel has been used by us often as a source—the tight bunches of fruits and the tiny background motif are very pleasing.

Left Sampler inspired by the Copeland Spode china

Right Mirror frame with its fabric inspiration

39

COPELAND SPODE PLATES

Finished size of designs: 7in (18cm) diameter
Tracings: pages 172/3

MATERIALS

COPELAND SPODE FRUIT PLATE
Appleton's crewel wool

Crimson	947	1 skein
Pale Green	421	1 skein
Dark Green	831	1 skein
Pale Blue	743	1 skein
Dark Blue	821	1 skein
Navy	747	1 skein
Pale Pink	711	1 skein
Dark Pink	713	1 skein
Purple	101	1 skein
Beige	762	1 skein
Yellow	472	1 skein

Anchor stranded cotton

Blue	0146	2 skeins
White	01	5 skeins

COPELAND SPODE FLOWER PLATE
Appleton's crewel wool

Crimson	947	1 skein
Pale Green	421	1 skein
Dark Green	831	1 skein
Pale Blue	743	1 skein
Dark Blue	821	1 skein
Navy	747	1 skein
Pale Pink	711	1 skein
Dark Pink	713	1 skein
Purple	101	1 skein
Beige	762	1 skein
Yellow	472	1 skein

Anchor stranded cotton

Blue	0146	2 skeins
White	01	4 skeins

White interlocked canvas, 18 holes to the inch
Canvas size: 11in (28in) square

cont on page 44

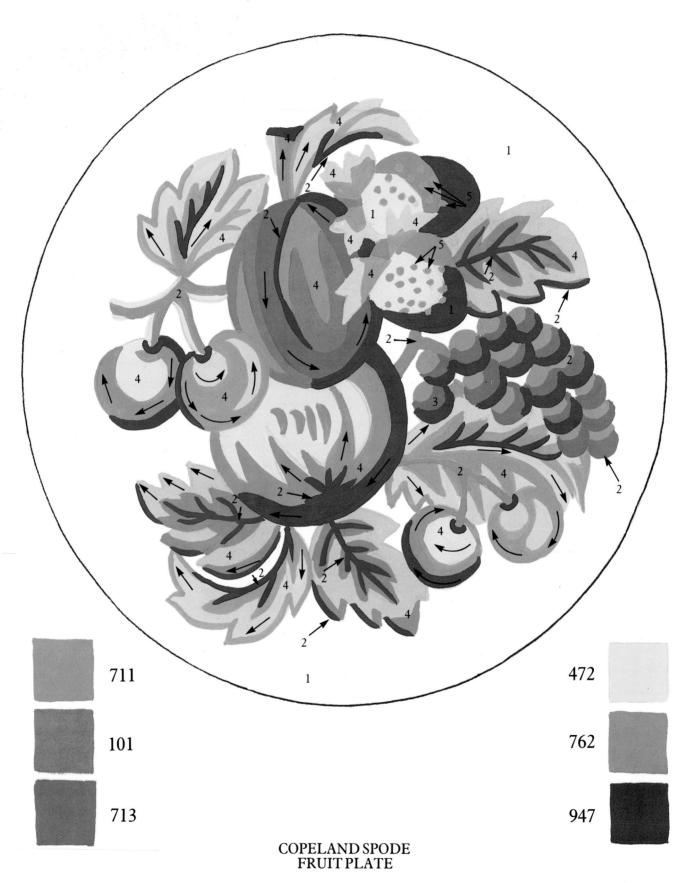

711

101

713

472

762

947

COPELAND SPODE
FRUIT PLATE

743

831

421

747

01

821+
0146

COPELAND SPODE
FLOWER PLATE

43

Size 22 needle
Compass
Ruler or tape measure
Masking tape for binding the canvas
Sharp scissors for cutting the canvas
Embroidery scissors
Sharp HB pencil or fine permanent marker in a suitable
  colour
Eraser

HOW TO MARK THE CANVAS
The same instructions apply to both designs.

Cut the canvas to size and tape the edges. Draw a 7in (18cm) circle with a compass or draw round a plate measuring the correct size. Trace the design (pages 172/3) onto the middle of the circle using a permanent marker or HB pencil. It is only necessary to trace the thick lines. The thin lines denote the change of colour and can be drawn freehand afterwards. Alternatively, trace the fine lines on in another colour.

HOW TO STITCH
Crewel wool has been used on these designs. Stranded cotton has only been used for the background and the white highlights on the flowers. Use two strands of crewel wool and six strands (the whole thread) of stranded cotton.

Stitches used
1 tent stitch
2 split back stitch
3 satin stitch
4 long and short stitch
5 French knots

The stitch cards will show you how to do the stitches. The numbers on the drawings (pages 42/3) refer to the numbers on the stitch cards. Refer to the colour drawing to show you which colour goes where and the direction of the stitches. The arrows show you the direction.

COPELAND SPODE FRUIT PLATE
All the navy outlining, veins and stalks, have been worked in SPLIT BACK stitch (2). The fruit has been stitched in LONG AND SHORT stitch (4); with the exception of the grapes which are in vertical SATIN stitch (3) edged in SPLIT BACK stitch (2) and the strawberries which are in TENT stitch (1); seeds in FRENCH KNOTS (5). The stems are also in SPLIT BACK stitch (2). LONG AND SHORT stitch (4) has also been used for the leaves.

COPELAND SPODE FLOWER BASKET
All the navy outlining, veins, stamens, stems and edging on the basket have been worked in SPLIT BACK stitch (2). The flowers are in LONG AND SHORT stitch (4) with single SATIN stitches (3) and FRENCH KNOTS (5) in the centre. The grapes are in vertical SATIN stitch (3) edged in SPLIT BACK stitch (2). The leaves are in SATIN stitch (3) and LONG AND SHORT stitch (4). The basket is in horizontal SATIN stitch (3).

THE BACKGROUND OF THE TWO DESIGNS
Work the blue motifs randomly, fairly close together, over the background, in TENT stitch (1) in blue stranded cotton—see Diagram 1 on how to do each motif. Finally work the background in white stranded cotton TENT stitch (1).

If you would like to adapt your own china to needlework, copy the outline of the design onto a piece of paper and enlarge it if necessary. Follow the colours from the china.

These designs were taken from Copeland Spode china (pattern George III), dated 1908.

MAKING UP INSTRUCTIONS
After the designs have been sewn it may be necessary to stretch them back into shape (see Chapter 15). You may prefer to take your work to a professional framer to finish it and they will then stretch it for you.

**THE BACKGROUND
MOTIF**

Right Colefax and
Fowler's Tree Poppies
chintz, shown adapted as
a cushion and bell pull

TREE POPPIES

Finished size of design: 12in × 10in (31 × 26cm)
Tracings: pages 174/5

In adapting the Colefax & Fowler Tree Poppies, we have intentionally softened the colours slightly. Appleton's wools have such an enormous range that matching is almost always successful. However, using a much smaller palette—nine colours as opposed to sixteen of the fabric, the balance had to be adjusted.

MATERIALS
Appleton's tapestry wool

White	991	⅓ hank (24 × 30in/75cm lengths)
Pale Pink	751	½ hank (36 × 30in/75cm lengths)
Pale Terracotta	222	¾ hank (54 × 30in/75cm lengths)
Med Terracotta	224	¾ hank (54 × 30in/75cm lengths)
Dark Terracotta	226	¼ hank (18 × 30in/75cm lengths)
Pale Blue	886	½ hank (36 × 30in/75cm lengths)
Med Blue	321	½ hank (36 × 30in/75cm lengths)
Dark Blue	323	¼ hank (18 × 30in/75cm lengths)
Beige	761	½ hank (36 × 30in/75cm lengths)
Cream	881	1½ hank (108 × 30in/75cm lengths)

White interlocked canvas, 14 holes to the inch
Canvas size: 16in × 14in (41 × 36cm)
Size 20 needle
Ruler or tape measure and eraser
Masking tape for binding the canvas
Sharp scissors for cutting the canvas
Embroidery scissors
Sharp HB pencil or fine permanent marker in a suitable
  colour

HOW TO MARK THE CANVAS
Cut the canvas to size and tape the edges.

Trace the design (pages 174/5) centrally onto the canvas and draw a line around it on the thread of the canvas. The red lines are the outside edges of the flowers and leaves. The black lines are to show a change in the shade of wool. If you are confident, copy the fine lines freehand in another colour. Otherwise, these can be traced on afterwards.

HOW TO STITCH
Use the whole thread throughout.

Stitches used
1 tent stitch
2 back stitch
3 satin stitch
4 long and short stitch
5 French knots
13 brick stitch over two threads

The stitch cards will show you how to do the stitches. The numbers on the coloured drawing refer to the numbers on the stitch cards. Refer to the colour photo and the drawing to show which colour goes where and the direction of the stitches. The arrows show the direction of the BRICK stitch (13). Refer to the colour photograph for the direction of the SATIN stitches.

Begin by stitching the poppies in LONG AND SHORT stitch (4) radiating out from the centre with the centres in TENT stitch (1). The stamens are FRENCH KNOTS (5) and single SATIN stitches (3). The other flowers are worked in LONG AND SHORT stitch (4) and SATIN stitch (3) radiating out from the centres, FRENCH KNOTS (5), and some outlining in BACK stitch (2). The leaves are in BRICK stitch (13) over two threads vertically or horizontally (13); veins and stems are in BACK stitch (2). The bamboo is worked in SATIN stitch (3) and the small beige leaves are worked in TENT stitch (1). The background is sewn in cream TENT stitch (1). Sew a line of mid-blue TENT stitch around the design.

This design is also perfect for a bell pull. Just decide how wide the bell pull is to be. First draw the outline and trace the various motifs onto a piece of tracing paper. Change the positions until you are satisfied. The drawing could be reduced if you wanted a narrow bell pull.

MAKING UP INSTRUCTIONS
After the design has been sewn it may be necessary to stretch it back into shape (Chapter 15) and then you can make it into a cushion (see Chapter 15 also).

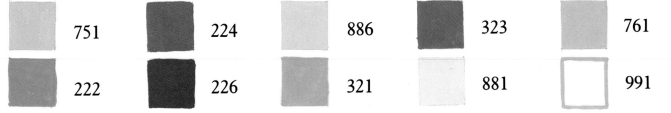

751

224

886

323

761

222

226

321

881

991

TREE POPPIES

INTERWOVEN RIBBONS

Finished size of design: 11½in sq (29cm)
Tracings: pages 176/7

The 'ribbons' idea can be very versatile. In this case, it was necessary to play around with the ribbons for some time until the ratio of pattern to stripe looked balanced—not only the colours, but the fussiness of the flowers against the regimentation of the stripes.

MATERIALS
Appleton's tapestry wool

Pale Pink	751	¾ hank (54 × 30in/75cm lengths)
Mid Pink	754	¾ hank (54 × 30in/75cm lengths)
Dark Pink	944	– (3 × 30in/75cm lengths)
Very Pale Green	873	½ hank (36 × 30in/75cm lengths)
Peppermint Green	432	½ hank (36 × 30in/75cm lengths)
Emerald Green	435	¾ hank (54 × 30in/75cm lengths)
Leaf Green	423	¾ hank (54 × 30in/75cm lengths)
Blue	741	⅓ hank (24 × 30in/75cm lengths)
Yellow	841	¾ hank (54 × 30in/75cm lengths)
White	991	– (3 × 30in/75cm lengths)

Far left Interwoven Ribbons, four Designers Guild fabrics in one cushion. Each fabric keeps its own personality within the overlapping ribbon sections

Left The fabrics and friezes that inspired the Interwoven Ribbons cushion

49

White mono deluxe canvas, 14 holes to the inch
Canvas size: 15½ins sq (40cm)
Size 20 needle
Ruler or tape measure
Masking tape for binding the canvas
Sharp scissors for cutting the canvas
Embroidery scissors
Sharp HB pencil or fine permanent marker in a suitable
  colour
Eraser

HOW TO MARK THE CANVAS

Cut the canvas to size and bind the edges. With an HB pencil mark out the canvas starting at the top right-hand corner, approximately 2in (5cm) from the edge of the canvas—see Diagram 1 and the colour chart. Count the holes carefully and draw the lines following the thread of the canvas. When you have finished marking, erase the unnecessary lines—see Diagram 2, which shows the interwoven ribbons. Mark out the ribbons with a permanent marker in an appropriate colour.

Trace the flowers pages 176/7) onto the ribbons using a permanent marker, taking care to position them correctly. The same drawing is used for both the flowery ribbons B. Just turn the drawing upside down to trace. Use the colour picture of the cushion and the colour chart as your guide.

HOW TO STITCH THE DESIGN

Use the whole thread throughout.

Stitches used

1 tent stitch
2 back stitch
3 satin stitch
4 long and short stitch
5 French knots

The stitch cards will show you how to do the stitches. Refer to the colour chart and the colour picture for the colour of the wool, position and direction of the stitches. The numbers refer to the stitch card numbers.

Begin by stitching the flowers in SATIN stitch (3) and LONG AND SHORT stitch (4).   The veins on the leaves and the stems have been worked in SPLIT BACK stitch (2). Some outlining of the flowers and the stamens are also in SPLIT BACK stitch (2): the ends of the stamens are FRENCH KNOTS (5). The leaves are in diagonal SATIN stitch (3). The background of the flowery ribbons is in A—yellow TENT stitch (1) continental. B—very pale green TENT stitch (1) continental. C—the striped ribbons are in TENT stitch (1) vertical. D—the plaid ribbon is in diagonal SATIN stitch (3) and TENT stitch (1) continental. E—the two-tone green gingham check squares are in TENT stitch (1).

If you want to adapt this design to fit a large chair or stool, simply repeat more ribbons in the same proportion and retrace the flowers.

MAKING UP INSTRUCTIONS

After you have finished sewing, stretch the design and make into a cushion – see Chapter 15.

BEGIN HERE ⌐

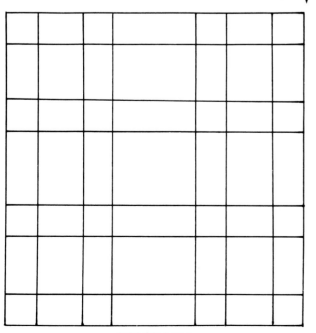

DIAGRAM 1

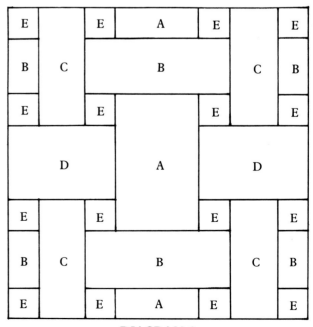

DIAGRAM 2

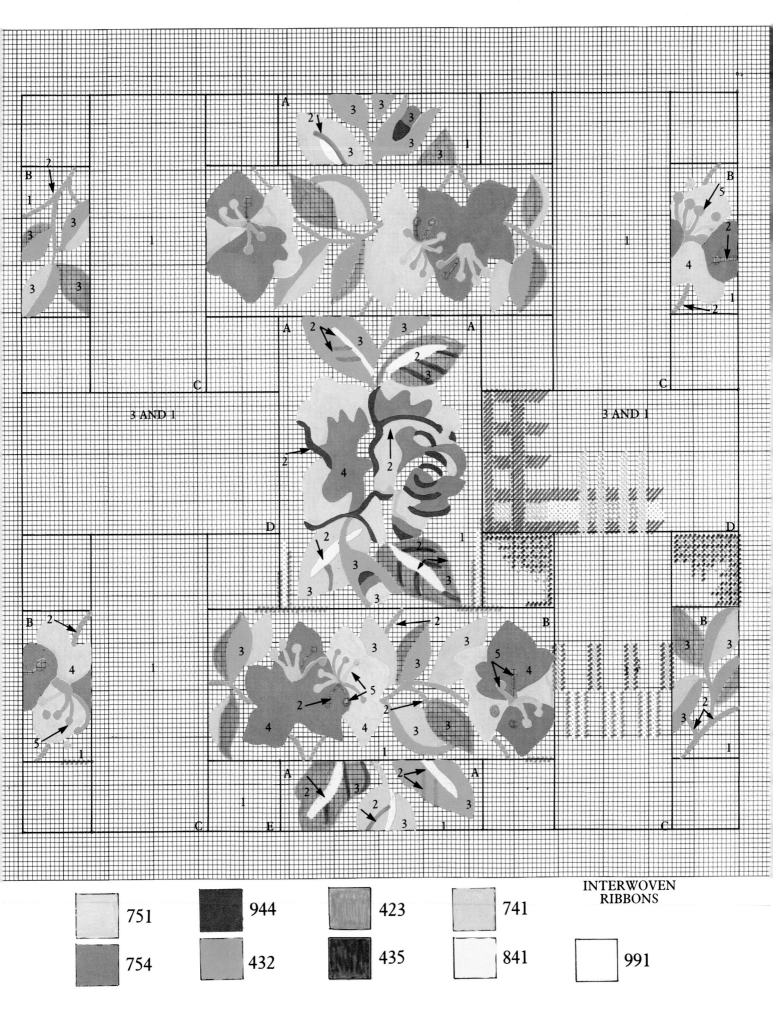

INTERWOVEN
RIBBONS

751	944	423	741
754	432	435	841	991

CHAPTER 4
THE BRITISH MUSEUM COLLECTION

In 1980 we were asked to design a canvas to commemorate the Viking Exhibition at the British Museum. In fact the canvas—inspired by the celebrated memorial-stones—designed itself; the intricate motifs, depictions of gods and men, duels and ceremonies, fell perfectly into place. Although we used source material without colour the rich browns and reds were taken from fragments of tapestry, found in Osberg, that show evidence of those colours. This is probably one of the most challenging designs to work—even so, we sold many thousands. The British *Times Business News* published a piece querying, 'What is this thing called needlepoint? Who are these women?'

As dutiful London parents, the Egyptian Rooms at the British Museum were de rigueur. Knowing that there are several ways to bring up children and all are wrong, we decided early on to strike places we found boring off the visiting list. Happily, our various children loved the Egyptian Rooms; we loved the Egyptian Rooms. The coffee shop was good. There were postcards, ice creams and pigeons . . . so started the interest—no, let's be more precise—the obsession, with the decorative elements of the Egyptians in general and the coffins in particular. The colours for a start, the geometry, the clarity and intricacy of the interlocking patterns were a joy to interpret first onto paper, then onto canvas, quite aside from their significance. Around the time the fascination was getting under way, Heather Dean from British Museum Publications —with perfect timing—asked, had we considered the Egyptians as a theme? Thus began Glorafilia's most enriching collaboration so far.

Aficionados of the British Museum, those of us who have an ongoing love affair with the place, need no explanation about how exciting working there can be. There is something magical about it. How

Right The Egyptian Tapestry from the British Museum Collection uses decorative elements from New Kingdom coffins 1500–1000 BC

Overleaf The forerunners of the British Museum Collection: (clockwise from the left) Etruscan, Viking, Egyptian, Islamic, Turkish, Anglo-Saxon and Japanese, photographed on the Museum steps

can such huge proportions be welcoming and human, when by rights they should feel intimidating? It always seems that the warmth of ghosts past live quite happily in those vaulted halls.

Designing the Ming Parrots for this book gave a delicious déjà vu feeling. Walking again those stone floors, looking for exactly the right thing, one stops seeing objects as something to be admired and, with the 'needlepoint mind' engaged, starts computing in terms of thread and stitch on canvas. The piece chosen is from the Ming dynasty, a cloisonné enamel box, decorated with parrots from the late fifteenth- early sixteenth-century AD, which interpets beautifully—the colours are in solid blocks outlined in gold (see page 60). You can look for a long time until something seems right—when it does, look no further.

It was decided that the designs that formed the basis for the British Museum Collection should be thematic composites gathered from as many treasures as necessary within the museum—literally 'archival' stuff. The experience was wonderful and it was a great privilege to see behind the famous façade. The designs were submitted to the museum scholars for close scrutiny—no artistic licence was permissible—to get an original distillation of five chosen themes.

The five pieces chosen were a Turkish picture based on an Iznik pottery dish dated 1540–50 which we loved for the richness of its colour. The Islamic design was based on sixteenth- and seventeenth-century paintings from Rajasthan and from Deccan and Mughal schools (sixteenth century). The

The Vikings, the first of the British Museum designs, inspired by the celebrated memorial stones. It depicts gods and men, duels and ceremonies and is bordered by intricate interlacing and classical motifs

mingling of exotic decorative styles drawn from the wide Islamic empire, gave this art its unique character, designed for pure visual delight. Glorious!

The Japanese design, based on eighteenth-century prints by Shumman and Ejiki, demonstrates again how perfectly Japanese prints, with their outlining and simplicity of flat colour, adapt to needlepoint. The Etruscan design shows Pegasus and details from Greek red and black figure vases (500–400BC) which was an irresistible choice—the Etruscans were the first people to make statues of their gods and the development of the red and black vase schools of Ancient Greece are legendary.

And, of course, the Egyptian piece. The design was based on elements from New Kingdom coffins (1500–1000BC). The source material was rich; figures and objects were drawn or incised in elegant lines and brilliantly coloured. Even more interesting than the magnificent decorations was the human figure—drawn with head, arms and legs in profile, shoulders and torso in three-quarter view and the eye in full view—the Egyptians were not interested in realism and the flat, stylised drawings could not have been better to interpret onto canvas.

Since those first designs we have added a Greek and another Egyptian, then the British Museum persuaded us to design an Anglo-Saxon tapestry to coincide with the 1984 exhibition. We affectionately called it the 'Scrambled Egg and Tomato' design, and were not convinced of its success—how wrong we were. It has proved to be one of our most popular designs.

As Heather Dean said, 'They'll still be selling the Egyptian kit long after we're dead.' We dismissed the question of who would be producing it.

The British Museum Greek design, showing Triptolemos in his winged chariot, holding ears of corn as a gift for mankind. Persephone offers him wine for a libation before the start of his journey. From a red-figured drinking cup by the Athenian artist Makron, about 490–480 BC

ΛΑΟΔΑΜΕΙΑ

ΘΗΣΕΥΣ

MING PARROTS

Finished size of design: 9½in (24cm) diameter
Tracing: page 179

Materials
Appleton's crewel wool

E	Emerald Green	831	2 skeins
Y	Yellow	472	2 skeins
R	Red	626	1 skein
T	Turquoise	524	4 skeins
F	Fawn	201	1 skein
B	Blue	923	1 skein
C	Cinnamon	766	2 skeins
Bk	Black	998	7 skeins
W	White	991	2 skeins

G Gold Astrella metallic embroidery thread (Coats)
11 skeins

White interlocked canvas, 18 holes to the inch
Canvas size: 14in × 14in (36cm)
Size 22 needle
Compass
Ruler or tape measure
Masking tape for binding the canvas
Sharp scissors for cutting the canvas
Embroidery scissors
Sharp HB pencil or fine permanent marker in a suitable
 colour
Eraser

HOW TO MARK THE CANVAS
Cut the canvas to size and tape the edges.
 Draw a 9½in (24cm) circle in the middle of the canvas. Use a compass or draw round a plate measuring the correct size.
 With a permanent marker, trace the design (page 179) onto the canvas. The thick lines denote where the gold thread is used. The dotted lines indicate where there is a change of colour. If possible, mark the design onto the canvas using two different colours to show the difference

HOW TO STITCH
Use two strands of crewel wool and two strands of gold thread throughout.

Stitches used
 1 tent stitch
 2 split back stitch
 3 satin stitch
 4 long and short stitch
13 vertical brick stitch (over two threads of canvas)

The stitch cards will show you how to do the stitches. The numbers on the diagram overleaf refer to the numbers on the stitch cards. Where this is no number, TENT stitch (1) has been used.
 The letters refer to the colours. The absence of a letter denotes a black background. All black areas are worked in TENT stitch (Bk1) including the pupils of the parrots' eyes.
 The red arrows show the direction of the stitches.

Right Ming Parrots –
adapted from a cloisonné
enamel box (left) from the
Ming Dynasty

The black thick lines are to be worked in gold thread in SPLIT BACK stitch (G2).

The tree trunk is worked vertically in cinnamon wool in BRICK stitch over two threads of canvas (C13).

The fine black lines are to show the direction of the SATIN stitches.

Work the gold thread first followed by the parrots. Then stitch the fruit, the leaves and the tree trunk.

Then sew in the black background. Leave the white on the parrot to the end.

If you are making up the design as we have, surround the design with two or three rows of extra TENT stitch (1) in black wool.

MAKING UP INSTRUCTIONS

After the design has been sewn it may be necessary to stretch it back to shape (Chapter 15) and then you can frame it or make it into a cushion (Chapter 15 again). If you decide to frame it, we suggest you take it to a professional framer, who will also stretch it for you.

MING PARROTS

CHAPTER 5
LEARN NEEDLEPOINT
THE GLORAFILIA WAY

For anyone who has ever said, 'I wouldn't know where to start!'—this is for you!

The Learn Needlepoint series began when we moved into the Old Mill House and planned to give needlepoint classes. This never happened for two reasons. The first was that in a shop already threatening to burst there was barely enough room for a customer to move freely, let alone to seat pupils. The second reason was that by the time we had completed the stitch cards, printed the working chart, designed, worked and photographed the

Below Rhodes stitch Photo-frame – clearly showing the subtle gradation of colour

Overleaf Selection of finished Learn Needlepoint Kits

samples, there was no need for a teacher. It was so self-explanatory that we just put the whole thing in a pack. There is a note in each kit saying that we have an open morning, a 'surgery' every Wednesday 10–1, in case anybody needs personal encouragement. Seven years on, hundreds of kits later, we can count on one hand those who have needed help.

The design (opposite) is one of the three Learn Needlepoint Kits. There are three different centres and three colourways and we give you a stitch guide, one step at a time. The beauty of its concept is that because the sections are small, you have the satisfaction of completing and mastering a stitch at a time, at your own pace, and this is instantly satisfying and immensely rewarding.

If you are designing your own needlepoint sampler, the main watchpoint is colour. Keep your palette of colours simple and the stitches won't disturb each other. The more colours, the more likelihood of disharmony. Your eye should be able to move happily around the finished design with nothing jumping out and shrieking. It's easy—and we all have done it—to stand in front of a mouth-watering display of wools and choose too many colours. Resist!

The design (opposite) illustrates what we mean by harmony. We have kept to three shading tones, plus cream, and a contrast colour. For an even subtler effect we could have used five shading tones of the same colour. However, adding the contrast spices up the design a little and prevents predictability. A never-forgotten lesson with paint was doing an entire picture using one colour and white; certainly, with wool, these same restrictions can be very interesting. Work out how many colours you are going to use. Start with three tones—light, medium and darker (remembering that wool always works up darker than it appears in the skein)—and then add intermediate tones and a contrast shade. As a general rule, if you use colours with the same tonal value together, there will be no contrast and the pattern-effect will be lost—although there are deliberate uses of this which are very valuable—see our comments about 'Morning, Volterra', page 104. However, when using different types of yarn in

the same tone, beautifully subtle effects can be achieved—try combining cotton, which reflects light, with wool, which absorbs light. There is no end to the interesting colour combinations you can use and at different times you will be drawn towards quite different hues. We have moved from earth colours, through ice cream colours and warm pastels, to dark Victorian tones. Let your imagination wander and see where it lands, and unless you have a specific colour scheme to fit into, reach into the shelves you normally wouldn't try. Look for contrasts among the pale tones of elephant grey, dull mauves, greeny-stones—they can have chameleon effects when placed with other colours and take on qualities you wouldn't expect to see. Avoid black—unless for specific dramatic effect—substitute instead, with no loss of depth, grey, Prussian blue, dull mauve, plum—they can bring a warmth that black doesn't have.

In the designs shown here, the sections opposite each other—either directly or diagonally—balance not only in colour, but in the size and textural quality of the stitch and this is another point to watch.

Learn Needlepoint teaches twenty-two different stitches—some you will put into your stitch repertoire and use constantly—the cards are there as 'refreshers' whenever you need them, so there is no need to memorise every stitch. Most of the stitches are geometric, but on the central motif of each is a taste of the more creative stitches—long and short stitch, satin stitch, back stitch and French knots. With these mastered—and there is nothing complicated about mastering them—you will soon be able to look at a picture and decide exactly what you want; a textured look in one place, movement in another, tent stitch in parts to recede, long and short stitch for the foliage, etc.

Learn Needlepoint gives you the tools for creating pictures and will give you the confidence to tackle them. Whatever you are working must be seen as a complete picture—however beautiful the stitches are, they are only an ingredient in the overall finished effect.

| *Right* Learn Needlepoint Fan

FAN, PEONY AND BUTTERFLY

Finished design size: 12in × 12in (31 × 31cm)
Tracings: pages 177/8

This is the original Glorafilia Learn Needlepoint Sampler, with twenty-two different stitches—there is a smaller, easier version on page 75.

MATERIALS
Appleton's tapestry wool

FAN
☐ Elephant Grey 971 1 hank (72 × 30in/75cm lengths)
◇ Old Rose   141 1 hank (72 × 30in/75cm lengths)
+ Sugar Pink   751 1 hank (72 × 30in/75cm lengths)
✳ Stone   988 1 hank (72 × 30in/75cm lengths)
√ White   991 1 hank (72 × 30in/75cm lengths)

PEONY
☐ Camel   761 1 hank (72 × 30in/75cm lengths)
◇ Old Gold   692 1 hank (72 × 30in/75cm lengths)
+ Orange   851 1 hank (72 × 30in/75cm lengths)
✳ Yellow   841 1 hank (72 × 30in/75cm lengths)
√ White   991 1 hank (72 × 30in/75cm lengths)

BUTTERFLY
☐ Terracotta   204 1 hank (72 × 30in/75cm lengths)
◇ Dusky Pink 121 1 hank (72 × 30in/75cm lengths)
+ Salmon Pink 708 1 hank (72 × 30in/75cm lengths)
✳ Peach   702 1 hank (72 × 30in/75cm lengths)
√ White   991 1 hank (72 × 30in/75cm lengths)

White mono deluxe canvas, 14 holes to the inch
Canvas size: 16in × 16in (41cm)
Size 20 needle
Masking tape for binding the canvas
Ruler or tape measure
Sharp scissors for cutting the canvas
Embroidery scissors
Sharp HB pencil or fine permanent marker in a suitable colour
Eraser

HOW TO MARK THE CANVAS
Cut the canvas to size and tape the edges.
Mark out the canvas using an HB pencil or permanent marker in a pale shade. The graph has been drawn to scale. Each square of the graph represents one hole of the canvas and the lines represent the threads. Count the squares and then draw the lines on the thread of the canvas with the exception of the red lines which should go between the thread. Mark on the solid lines and the dotted lines. Begin with the central square, the central border and then the smaller areas and the outer border, the chain stitch lines (between the threads) and then the broken lines. (NB the broken lines that denote the centre for the diamond eyelet are also between the threads.) Mark 'Top' on the canvas, as this will help when turning the canvas.

It is important to count accurately. If you do make a mistake, the pattern will not work out. Double check before continuing.

Trace the outline of the fan, peony, or butterfly (pages 177/8) onto the central square.

HOW TO STITCH
Use the whole thread throughout.

Stitches used

1	tent stitch	2	back stitch
3	satin stitch	4	long and short stitch
5	French knots	6	crossed corners
7	Parisian stitch	8	leaf stitch
9	Algerian eye stitch	10	Scottish stitch
11	knitting stitch	12	upright cross stitch
13	brick stitch	14	double cross stitch
15	continuous Scottish stitch	16	mosaic stitch
17	continuous mosaic stitch	18	2–4–6–8 tie stitch
19	chain stitch	20	border pattern
21	diamond eyelet stitch	22	long legged cross stitch

We have used twenty-two different stitches in this one design. Each version, 'Butterfly', 'Peony' or 'Fan' has the same stitch instruction but the instructions for the central motif and the colour key are obviously different.

The stitch cards will show you how to do the

FAN

751
141
971
991

PEONY

841
851
761
991

BUTTERFLY

702
708
204
991

stitches. The numbers refer to the numbers on the stitch cards.

For the position, colour and direction of the stitches, refer to the diagram and the colour picture. It may be necessary to use compensating stitches from time to time and we have shown how to do this on each stitch area in the diagram. When working a stitch in alternate colours a beginner may find it easier to finish at the end of the first row and re-thread the needle in the other colour when beginning the next row. Familiarise yourself with each stitch by sewing on the cards until you feel confident to begin the canvas.

Begin by sewing the central motif.

FAN

The pink background of the fan has been worked in TENT stitch (1) edged in BACK stitch (2). The flower is in LONG AND SHORT stitch (4) also edged in BACK stitch (2). We have used diagonal SATIN stitch (3) for the leaves and the stems are worked in BACK stitch (2). The base of the fan and the ribbon are sewn in vertical SATIN stitch (3) edged in BACK stitch (2). FRENCH KNOTS (5) have been used for the 'dots' on a white background of TENT stitch (1)—continental or basketweave.

PEONY

The peony has been worked in LONG AND SHORT stitch (4) with FRENCH KNOTS (5) for the centre. We have used horizontal, vertical and diagonal SATIN stitch (3) for the leaves—see the lines on the diagram and the colour photograph for the direction. The veins are in BACK stitch (2). The white background is in TENT stitch (1)—continental.

BUTTERFLY

We have used horizontal and vertical SATIN stitch (3) for the butterfly—see the lines on the diagram—with areas in LONG AND SHORT stitch (4) and FRENCH KNOTS (5) all edged in BACK stitch (2). The white background is in TENT stitch (1)—continental or basketweave.

THE STITCHERY AREA

When the centre is completely sewn, divide each stitch area on the lines with a line of TENT stitch (1) (continental or vertical) except for the outside line, which is LONG LEGGED CROSS stitch (22).

Then sew the border around the centre using CROSSED CORNERS (6). Working clockwise, turning the canvas as you go, stitch each area in numerical order beginning with PARISIAN stitch (7) and finishing with MOSAIC stitch (16). Begin in the corner shown on the diagram.

Starting at the top right of the canvas fill in the corner triangles with CONTINUOUS MOSAIC stitch (17) and 2–4–6–8 TIE (18). We have shown various stages of these stitches in each triangle.

Work the CHAIN stitch (19) beginning at the top right hand corner.

Sew the BORDER PATTERN (20) beginning at the centre right and then put in whole and half DIAMOND EYELET stitches (21) wherever the diamonds and triangles are formed. We have shown how to mitre the corners on the border (bottom right on the diagram).

Finally, surround the sampler with LONG LEGGED CROSS stitch (22), beginning at the bottom left hand corner and sewing from left to right.

MAKING UP INSTRUCTIONS

When you have finished sewing, the design will need to be stretched (see Chapter 15) and made into a cushion (Chapter 15 also).

Diagram key
——— CHAIN stitch
– – – – Break of pattern except where it is the central position of the border (marked centre).
——— TENT stitch except for the outside line which is LONG LEGGED CROSS stitch
←—— Direction of stitching.

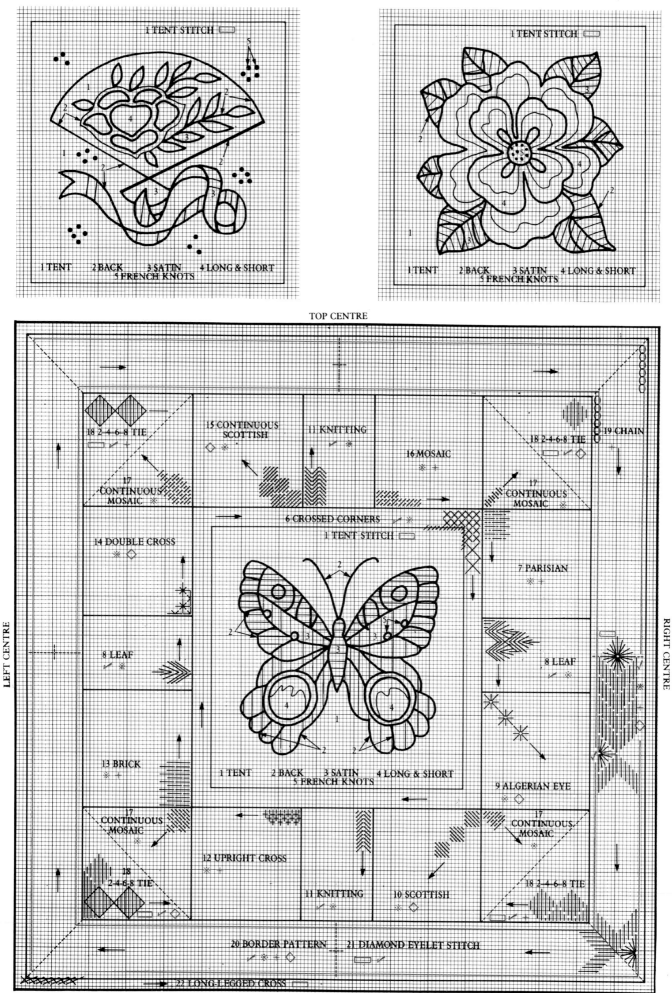

1 TENT STITCH

1 TENT   2 BACK   3 SATIN   4 LONG & SHORT
5 FRENCH KNOTS

1 TENT STITCH

1 TENT   2 BACK   3 SATIN   4 LONG & SHORT
5 FRENCH KNOTS

TOP CENTRE

LEFT CENTRE

RIGHT CENTRE

18 2-4-6-8 TIE

15 CONTINUOUS
SCOTTISH

11 KNITTING

16 MOSAIC

18 2-4-6-8 TIE   19 CHAIN

17
CONTINUOUS
MOSAIC

17
CONTINUOUS
MOSAIC

14 DOUBLE CROSS

6 CROSSED CORNERS

1 TENT STITCH

7 PARISIAN

8 LEAF

8 LEAF

13 BRICK

1 TENT   2 BACK   3 SATIN   4 LONG & SHORT
5 FRENCH KNOTS

9 ALGERIAN EYE

17
CONTINUOUS
MOSAIC

17
CONTINUOUS
MOSAIC

18
2-4-6-8 TIE

12 UPRIGHT CROSS

11 KNITTING   10 SCOTTISH

18 2-4-6-8 TIE

20 BORDER PATTERN   21 DIAMOND EYELET STITCH

22 LONG-LEGGED CROSS

BOTTOM CENTRE

PHOTOGRAPH FRAME

Size: 7in × 8½in (18 × 22cm)

Colours: 2A Green Colourway
2B Pink Colourway
2C Yellow Colourway
2D Blue Colourway

MATERIALS
Appleton's tapestry wool
DMC coton perlé No 3

2A GREEN
Tapestry wool
P Pale Green 521 1 hank (72 × 30in/75cm lengths)
M Med Green 641 ¾ hank (54 × 30in/75cm lengths)
D Dark Green 642 ½ hank (36 × 30in/75cm lengths)
Coton Perlé
B Br Green 502 2 skeins

2B PINK
Tapestry wool
P Pale Pink 751 1 hank (72 × 30in/75cm lengths)
M Med Pink 753 ¾ hank (54 × 30in/75cm lengths)
D Dark Pink 754 ½ hank (36 × 30in/75cm lengths)
Coton perlé
B Bright Pink 899 2 skeins

2C YELLOW
Tapestry wool
P Pale Yellow 871 1 hank (72 × 30in/75cm lengths)
M Med Yellow 872 ¾ hank (54 × 30in/75cm lengths)
D Dark Yellow 841 ½ hank (36 × 30in/75cm lengths)
Coton perlé
B Bright Yellow 745 2 skeins

2D BLUE
Tapestry wool
P Pale Blue 886 1 hank (72 × 30in/75cm lengths)
M Med Blue 742 ¾ hank (54 × 30in/75cm lengths)
D Dark Blue 744 ½ hank (36 × 30in/75cm lengths)
Coton perlé
B Bright Blue 799 2 skeins

White mono deluxe canvas, 14 holes to the inch
Canvas size: 11in × 12½in (28 × 32cm)
Size 20 needle
Masking tape for binding canvas
Ruler or tape measure
Sharp HB pencil or permanent marker in a suitable colour
Sharp scissors for cutting the canvas
Embroidery scissors
Eraser

It is not necessary to mark out the canvas, just follow the chart overleaf.

HOW TO STITCH
Three rows of RHODES stitch (24) have been worked over a seven thread square together with four rows of TENT stitch (1) in the centre and on the outside of the frame. The effect of the raised shaded rows and the lustre of the coton perlé is very attractive and perfect for the photograph frame as it does not detract from the photograph.

The whole thread is used throughout.

Stitches used
1 tent stitch
24 Rhodes stitch

The stitch cards will show you how to do the stitches. Refer to the diagram overleaf for the position and direction of the stitches. The arrows refer to the direction of working. The letters refer to the colours, and the numbers refer to the stitch card numbers.

We have shown how to stitch the frames vertically, but once sewn they can be used horizontally.

Start approximately 3½in (9cm) from the edge of the canvas and begin by working nine RHODES stitches (24) horizontally in the darkest shade of wool (D). Work from right to left. Begin each row as shown on the diagram.

| *Right* Rhodes stitch Photo-frames

Sew a row of twelve RHODES stitches vertically (the first RHODES stitch will already have been worked). Complete the oblong in the dark wool (D24), nine stitches at the top and bottom, twelve at the sides.

Follow this by sewing a row of RHODES stitches in the medium shade (M24) all around the dark shade, eleven at the top and bottom, fourteen at the sides. Then work the third row in the palest shade (P24), thirteen at the top and bottom and sixteen at the sides.

Finally, sew four rows of TENT stitch in coton perlé (B1) around the centre and on the outside.

This design can be adapted to a cushion design. There are great possibilities for shading using different yarns.

MAKING UP INSTRUCTIONS

When you have finished sewing, the photo-frame may need to be stretched (see Chapter 15) and made into a frame—see Chapter 15 also.

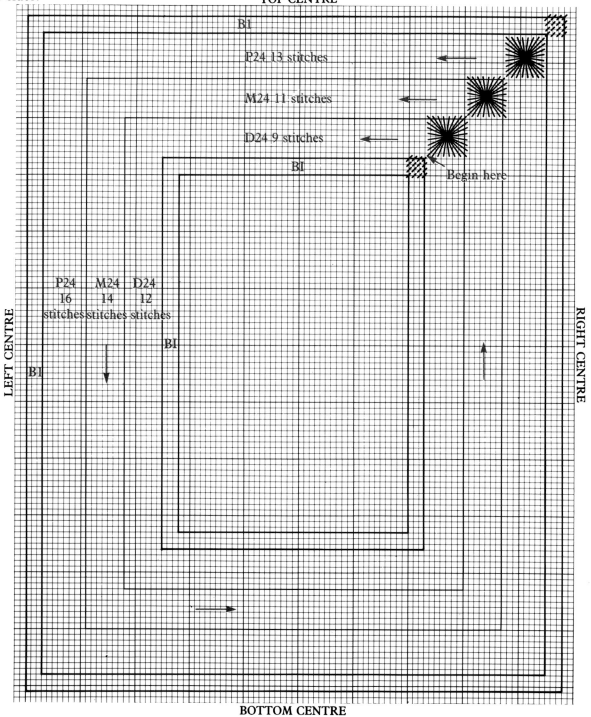

DIAMOND STITCHERY

Size: 8in × 8in (20 × 20cm)
Colours: pink-green, peach/grey

MATERIALS
Appleton's tapestry wool

PINK/GREEN
√ White   991 ¾ hank (54 × 30in/75cm lengths)
✳ Pale Pink   751 ½ hank (36 × 30in/75cm lengths)
+ Sugar Pink 941 ¾ hank (54 × 30in/75cm lengths)
◇ Shocking
     Pink   943 ⅓ hank (24 × 30in/75cm lengths)
☐ Green   641 ½ hank (36 × 30in/75cm lengths)

PEACH/GREY
√ White   991 ¾ hank (54 × 30in/75cm lengths)
✳ Pale Peach 703 ½ hank (36 × 30in/75cm lengths)
+ Peach   621 ¾ hank (54 × 30in/75cm lengths)
◇ Coral   622 ⅓ hank (24 × 30in/75cm lengths)
☐ Grey   963 ½ hank (36 × 30in/75cm lengths)

White mono deluxe canvas, 14 holes to the inch
Canvas size: 12in × 12in (31 × 31cm)
Size 20 needle
Ruler or tape measure
Masking tape for binding the canvas
Sharp scissors for cutting the canvas
Embroidery scissors
Sharp HB pencil or fine permanent marker in a suitable
    colour
Eraser

HOW TO MARK THE CANVAS
Cut the canvas to size and tape the edges. Mark out the canvas using an HB pencil or permanent marker in a pale shade. The graph has been drawn to scale. Each square of the graph represents one hole of the canvas and the lines represent the threads. Count the squares and then draw the lines on the thread of the canvas with the exception of the red horizontal and vertical lines which should go between the thread. Begin by marking a small square in the centre of the canvas to cover 1 hole. Then count outwards and draw the central square in red (red on chart and between the lines). Then mark on the

diamond in red. (On the 'under' and 'over' of the canvas threads—see Fig 3 on page 13 in General Facts.) Mark the inner border and finally the outer border. Put in the broken lines (the broken lines that denote the centre for the DIAMOND EYELET are also between the threads). Mark 'Top' on the canvas—it will help if you need to turn the canvas.

It is extremely important to count accurately. If you make a mistake the pattern will not work out. Double check before continuing.

Trace the initial you require from Chapter 15 onto the central square of the canvas.

HOW TO STITCH
Use one strand of yarn throughout (the whole thread).

Stitches used
1	tent stitch	13	brick stitch
2	split back stitch		over two threads
6	crossed corners	19	chain stitch
7	Parisian stitch	20	border pattern
9	Algerian eye stitch	21	diamond eyelet stitch
10	Scottish stitch	22	long legged
			cross stitch

This is a smaller and easier version of the large Learn Needlepoint sampler that uses twenty-two different stitches. The border has been adapted from the BORDER PATTERN (20) and is slightly reduced in size. BRICK stitch (13) is worked over two threads of canvas, not four as on the card. We have used an initial for the centre, but you could put a date or a name, see pages 186/7, to commemorate a birthday, anniversary, etc. Or you can think of an original motif.

For the position, colour and direction of the stitches, refer to the diagram overleaf and the colour photograph. The numbers refer to the numbers on the stitch cards. It may be necessary to use compensating stitches from time to time and we have shown how to do this on each stitch area in the diagram. When working a stitch in alternate colours a beginner may find it easier to finish at the end of the first row and re-thread the needle in the other colour when beginning the next row.

Begin stitching in the corner shown on the diagram. Sew the initial in the contrast colour in split BACK stitch (2). Work the CHAIN stitch (19) around the square and on the diamond. Then sew the white background of the central square which has been worked in TENT stitch (1)—basket weave. Sew the triangles between the CHAIN stitch (19) in

Diagram key
———— CHAIN stitch
– – – – break of pattern except where it is the central position of the border (marked centre)
———— TENT stitch
◄——— direction of stitching

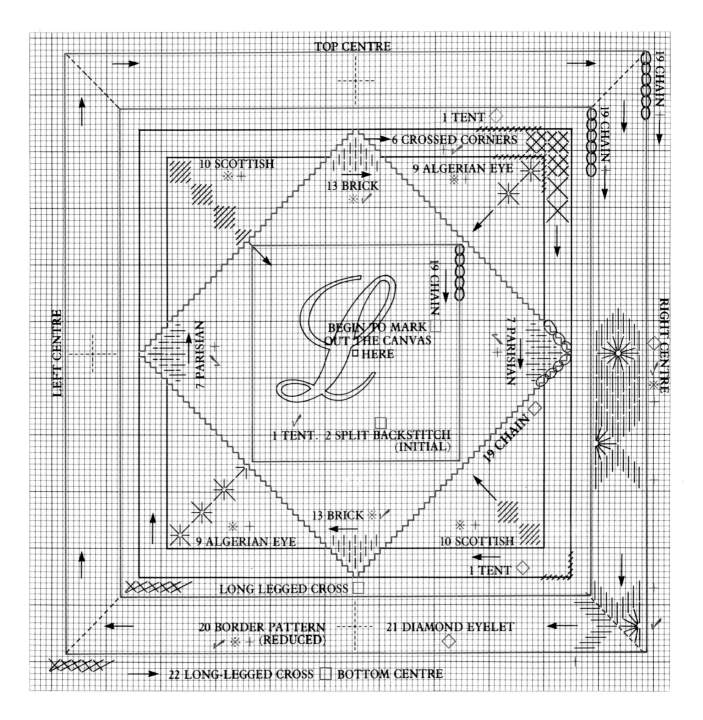

PARISIAN stitch (7) and BRICK stitch (13). Then work the TENT stitch (1) on either side of the CROSSED CORNERS (6) border. Sew the outer triangles in SCOTTISH stitch (10) and ALGERIAN EYE stitch (9). Put in the CROSSED CORNERS (6) between the tent stitch. Sew a line of LONG LEGGED CROSS (22), working from left to right in the contrast colour outside the crossed corners border. Work the CHAIN stitch (19) surrounding the outer border beginning at the top right hand corner.

Sew the BORDER PATTERN (20) beginning at the centre right and then put in whole and half DIAMOND EYELET stitches (21) wherever the diamonds and triangles are formed. We have shown how to mitre the corners on the border—bottom right on the diagram. Finally, surround the sampler with LONG LEGGED CROSS stitch (22) beginning at the bottom left hand corner, sewing from left to right.

MAKING UP INSTRUCTIONS
When you have finished sewing the design, stretch back into shape (see Chapter 15) and make into a cushion (see Chapter 15 also).

MISTY ANEMONES

Finished size of design: 9in × 11in (23 × 28cm)
Tracing: page 181

MATERIALS
DMC coton perlé No 5

T	Taupe	640	1 skein
B	Beige	644	2 skeins
R	Rust	407	1 skein
N	Navy	823	1 skein
PP	Pale Pink	819	1 skein
L	Lilac	778	1 skein
M	Mushroom	842	1 skein
S	Silver Grey	762	2 skeins
E	Ecru		2 skeins

Appleton's crewel wool

P	Peach	877	4 skeins
H	Heather	883	3 skeins

White mono deluxe canvas, 18 holes to the inch
Size of canvas: 13in × 15in (33 × 38cm)
Size 22 needle
Ruler or tape measure
Masking tape for binding the canvas
Sharp scissors for cutting the canvas
Embroidery scissors
Sharp HB pencil or fine permanent marker in a suitable
  colour
Eraser

HOW TO MARK THE CANVAS
Cut the canvas to size and tape the edges.

Mark out the canvas using an HB pencil or permanent marker in a pale shade. The chart has been drawn to scale. Each square of the graph represents one hole of the canvas and the lines represent the threads. Count the squares and then draw the horizontal and vertical lines on the thread of the canvas. The diagonal lines should follow either the 'under' or 'over' threads—see how to mark the canvas in the General Information section. Double check that you have marked the canvas accurately. If you have made a mistake, the pattern will not work out.

Refer to the colour picture and the chart and trace the anemones and leaves (from page 181) onto the canvas, taking care to position them carefully. Erase the lines that go between the flowers, berries or leaves—see dotted lines on chart.

HOW TO STITCH
2 strands of crewel wool have been used; 1 whole thread of coton perlé.

Stitches used
 1 tent stitch
 2 split back stitch
 3 satin stitch

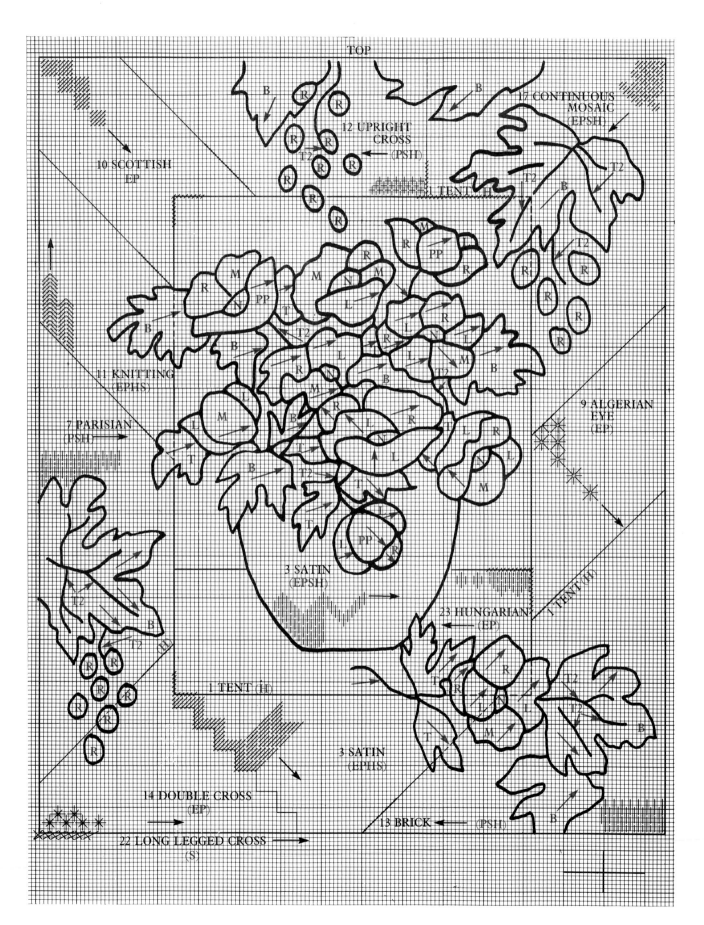

TOP

10 SCOTTISH
EP

12 UPRIGHT
CROSS
(PSH)

17 CONTINUOUS
MOSAIC
(EPSH)

1 TENT (H)

11 KNITTING
(EPHS)

9 ALGERIAN
EYE
(EP)

7 PARISIAN
(PSH)

3 SATIN
(EPSH)

23 HUNGARIAN
(EP)

1 TENT (H)

1 TENT (H)

3 SATIN
(EPHS)

13 BRICK   (PSH)

14 DOUBLE CROSS
(EP)

22 LONG LEGGED CROSS
(S)

7 Parisian stitch
9 Algerian eye stitch
10 Scottish stitch
11 knitting stitch
12 upright cross stitch
13 brick stitch
14 double cross stitch
17 continuous mosaic stitch
22 long legged cross stitch
23 Hungarian stitch

The stitch cards will show you how to do the stitches. The numbers refer to the numbers on the stitch cards.

For the position, colour and direction of the stitches, refer to the chart and the colour picture. It may be necessary to use compensating stitches from time to time. When working a stitch in alternate colours, a beginner may find it easier to finish at the end of the first row and re-thread the needle in the other colour when beginning the next row. Familiarise yourself with each stitch by sewing on the cards until you feel confident enough to begin the canvas. Where there is no number, SATIN stitch has been used.

Begin by sewing the anemones, berries and leaves in diagonal SATIN stitch (3). The arrows show the direction of the stitches. The veins and stems are in SPLIT BACK stitch (2). The vase is worked in vertical SATIN stitch (3) in a bargello pattern over three threads of canvas. The background has been left UNSEWN to give an added dimension to the design.

Divide each stitch area with heather TENT stitch (H1) on the lines marked on the canvas. (On the diagonal lines on the left side of the border we have reversed the direction of the TENT stitch to give an unbroken line.) The stepped line edging the bargello pattern at the bottom of the design has NOT been edged in TENT stitch. Nor has the line around the design.

Stitch the 'Tablecloth' in the centre in HUNGARIAN stitch (23).

Working clockwise, stitch each area starting with CONTINUOUS MOSAIC stitch (17) and ending with UPRIGHT CROSS stitch (12). Begin as shown on the diagram. Fill in with compensating stitches around the flowers and leaves.

Finally, surround the design with LONG LEGGED CROSS stitch in silver grey coton perlé (S22).

MAKING UP INSTRUCTIONS
After the design has been stitched, it may be necessary to stretch it back into shape (see Chapter 15) before making it into a picture or a cushion (again, see Chapter 15).

Left Misty Anemones, a very delicate picture, relying on stitchery for interest, and worked in coton perlé and crewel wool on 18 canvas. The background is left unworked to give another dimension. A good balance is achieved between the sleekness of the satin stitches and the textures of the smaller stitches

81

CHAPTER 6
JAPANESE INFLUENCES

We especially like Japanese themes and there are marvellously rich sources for ideas in eighteenth- and nineteenth-century prints, which were remarkable, not only in themselves, but for the tremendous influence they had on modern European painting. There is a flow and serenity about the work; delicacy and harshness, minute detail and sweeping dramatic gestures are all contained in a unique rhythm and harmony. These qualities make the prints perfect for needlepoint. The outlining typical of the woodblock prints, and the simple sections of colour, are a wonderful opportunity for varied stitchery. Once these outlined shapes are defined, the imagination can run away with itself.

Probably the most significant of our Japanese designs is 'Girl Playing Samisen' (overleaf): the figure was a woodblock print by Hokusai, the bamboo and fan elements were features we were using in various ways at that time, and the three fell together perfectly. Many years ago, in the pre-Glorafilia days, Carole painted this same figure on a huge scale on a very rough canvas to *imitate* a tapestry, to hang at the end of a theatrical hallway, flanked by two oriental tapestries. So we have taken a woodblock print and made it look like a tapestry and, twenty years on, created a tapestry to imitate the original woodblock print!

We love the tranquillity of this figure bending over her instrument. The initial impact of such a design is that it looks difficult to work. This is not true. Breaking down the design into sections and outlining, where necessary, to define areas of work completely stops any daunting aspect. Many people who have never worked in stitchery before have completed this successfully. The background uses a simple trick to give the appearance of a slub weave—just randomly stitch tent over two threads for an inch or two, and instead of being a blank and boring background it achieves depth. It's that simple.

'The Kabuki Actor' followed, using slightly more ambitious stitchery and pairing the 'Girl Playing Samisen' in colour and motifs. The blind in the background borders him on the right and the bamboo borders her on the left, making them look delightful together.

We rarely do faces in needlepoint, but adapting the face from Japanese art is different. There are no skin tones, just a flat area of white or cream, and the features are always portrayed in a minimal way, which suits needlework excellently. With a few lines an entire expression is suggested. Where Japanese designs do not show the face, this is not just for simplicity, but to convey an enigmatic quality. An averted head not only suggests the Japanese preference for privacy and shyness but also holds a fascination. This aspect, and the serenity of such subjects, makes them beautiful to work.

We were asked to design two large wall hangings for a compulsive stitcher who could never be without a piece of needlepoint in her hands and who

Right The Travellers – adapted from a print by Okumura Toshinobu

Overleaf Girl Playing Samisen, The Kabuki Actor and Wisteria — all worked in coton perlé

worked at an extraordinary speed. She needed something 'big' to get her teeth into. With 'The Travellers' (page 83), we played with stitches to make a marvellous mosaic of pattern within the picture. Stitchery gives this possibility as nothing else could—just see (opposite), how it brings another dimension to the work. The shaped stitches give dappled substance to the horse, the sweeping 'ink and brush' effect in the background contrasts well with the delicate aspects of her hands, feet and robe. The whole piece has the visual weight of a heavily woven tapestry and is deliciously tactile.

The second large piece was taken from an Utamaro print—from early in his series 'Poem of the Pillow'. It shows a couple making love on a balcony. He is watching her intently as she tenderly caresses his cheek. His hand is resting on the nape of her neck, an area of special erotic interest for the Japanese. His fan, held casually open, is inscribed with a poem that compares his position to a bird unable to fly away.

While researching the British Museum Collection, we asked to see any of this series that the museum owned. The series escalates in eroticism, and the prints, which were carefully taken from their folios and laid in front of us, would have given a whole new meaning to needlepoint! So we diplomatically stayed with these only slightly suggestive lovers who have now become part of our range.

The pair of cushions, 'Flowers and Fans' and 'Irises and Butterflies' (overleaf) are very delicate in feeling. The butterflies, fans and irises are from robes from the late Edo period; the camellias are taken from a waist sash (Koshi-obi). The stitches are quite simple, in keeping with the precision and clarity typical of Japanese art, where blooms and leaves were reduced to very simple patterns. The worked leaves sleekly imitate the silk of the original robes, and working the background in wool emphasises the sheen on the flowers and leaves. The stitchery border creates a harmonious edging to the picture with the 'discipline' appropriate to Japanese textiles, yet very much of today.

Right The Lovers, adapted from an Utamaro print, was first worked as a large wallhanging and later as a smaller picture for our collection. Both pieces have beautiful textural qualities

JAPANESE DESIGNS

Finished designs: 12½in × 10in (32 × 26cm)
Tracings: pages 182/3

MATERIALS

JAPANESE FLOWERS AND FANS
Anchor stranded cotton

C	Cream	926	5 skeins
P	Peach	778	5 skeins
T	Terracotta	868	2 skeins
O	Old Rose Pink	894	1 skein
R	Rust	883	1 skein
S	Sand	361	7 skeins
M	Mustard	943	2 skeins
B	Blue	848	3 skeins
A	Almond Green	858	4 skeins
G	Green	8581	2 skeins

Crewel wool
W White background 991 1 hank (72 30in/75cm lengths)

JAPANESE IRISES AND BUTTERFLIES
Anchor stranded cotton

C	Cream	926	5 skeins
P	Peach	778	5 skeins
T	Terracotta	868	2 skeins
O	Old Rose Pink	894	1 skein
R	Rust	883	1 skein
S	Sand	361	5 skeins
M	Mustard	943	1 skein
B	Blue	848	2 skeins
A	Almond Green	858	4 skeins
G	Green	8581	2 skeins

Crewel wool
W White background 991 1 hank (72 30in/75cm lengths)

Interlocked white canvas, 18 holes to the inch
Size of canvas: 17in × 14in (43 × 36cm)
Size 22 needle
Ruler or tape measure
Masking tape for binding the canvas
Sharp scissors for cutting the canvas
Embroidery scissors
Sharp HB pencil or fine permanent marker in a
    suitable colour
Eraser

FLOWERS AND FANS

BUTTERFLIES AND IRISES

HOW TO MARK THE CANVAS
The same instructions apply for both designs.

Cut the canvas to size and tape the edges. Place the drawing (pages 182/3) centrally under the canvas and trace the design. Draw the outline around the design, vertical and horizontal lines to be drawn *between* the thread of the canvas, corners curving. Measure a border of approximately 1½in (4cm) and draw another line *between* the threads of the canvas (no curves on the corners) see Diagram 1.

HOW TO STITCH
Six strands of stranded cotton (the whole thread) have been used throughout with the exception of the background of the central design when two strands of white crewel wool have been used.

Stitches used
1 tent stitch (single and double)
2 back stitch and split back stitch
3 satin stitch
4 long and short stitch
12 upright cross stitch
17 continuous mosaic stitch
19 chain stitch

The stitch cards will show you how to do the stitches. The numbers on the diagram refer to the numbers on the stitch cards. Where there is no number, tent stitch has been used. The letters refer to the colours. The arrows show the direction of the stitches.

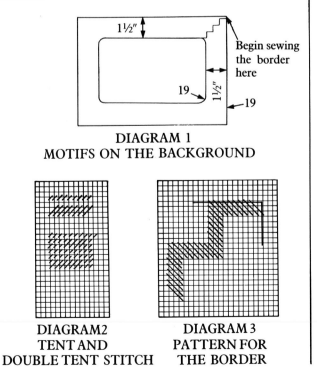

DIAGRAM 1
MOTIFS ON THE BACKGROUND

DIAGRAM 2
TENT AND
DOUBLE TENT STITCH

DIAGRAM 3
PATTERN FOR
THE BORDER

JAPANESE FLOWERS AND FANS
The flowers have been worked using LONG AND SHORT stitch (4) radiating out from the centre. The centres are sewn in UPRIGHT CROSS stitch (12). The leaves are in CONTINUOUS MOSAIC stitch (17) with the veins in SPLIT BACK stitch (2). The tree trunk is in diagonal SATIN stitch (3) over approximately four threads of canvas. Break the stitches at the dotted lines marked on the diagram. The branches are in SATIN stitch (3). The fans and ribbons are in TENT stitch (1), sticks in SPLIT BACK stitch (2) and the bottom of the fans are worked in vertical SATIN stitch (3). The background has been sewn in white crewel wool in TENT stitch (1) and an occasional band of double TENT stitch (1a) to give the effect of slub linen (see Diagram 2). The design has been outlined in CHAIN stitch (19).

JAPANESE IRISES AND BUTTERFLIES
The irises have been worked using LONG AND SHORT stitch (4) with some areas in diagonal SATIN stitch (3). The bamboo leaves are also in SATIN stitch (3) and the bottom of the flowers is sewn in CONTINUOUS MOSAIC stitch (17). The butterflies are in TENT stitch (1), antennae in BACK stitch (2). The background has been sewn in crewel wool in TENT stitch (1) and an occasional band of double TENT stitch (1a) to give the effect of slub linen—(see Diagram 2). The design has been outlined in CHAIN stitch (19).

THE BORDER FOR BOTH DESIGNS
The border has been worked using SATIN stitch in alternating colours of cream (C), peach (P), sand (S) and a few random rows of almond green (A) at the top left hand corner of the 'Flowers and Fans' and the bottom right hand corner of the 'Irises and Butterflies'.

Begin sewing the border at the top right hand corner of the design and work clockwise following Diagrams 1 and 3. The stitch is worked over three threads of canvas and changes from vertical to horizontal after nine stitches. Refer to the picture of the cushions to see where to put the almond green.

Finally, outline the entire design in another row of CHAIN stitch (19).

MAKING UP INSTRUCTIONS
When you have finished sewing, the designs may need to be stretched back into shape (see Chapter 15). They can then be made up into a cushion (also Chapter 15), alternatively they can be framed as a picture.

CHAPTER 7
MEDIEVAL

Tapestry has been called a 'mirror of history', and there are references to this art dating back to biblical times. However, it is the European medieval period from which we have drawn most of our inspiration. Western Europe had long been famed for its woven fabrics ('Weavers of Gaul rivalled those of Babylon and Alexandria') and by the fourteenth century it was regarded as a major art form. Designs covered all manner of subjects—classical, biblical, rural—initially in a flat, somewhat stylised form and later becoming more like a picture painted in thread, showing facial variation, movement and perspective. Perhaps the most beautiful examples came from Flanders and France. At one time, Paris was the acknowledged centre, and later this accolade passed to Arras whose name became synonymous with the craft. There was great demand for hangings of immense size, as well as small strips to hang between windows (entre fenêtre) and over doorways (fortières)—no insulation or central heating in those baronial halls.

Canvaswork is now often called tapestry, although this is really a misnomer. Canvaswork embroidery dates back to the sixteenth century coming to a peak during the late seventeenth and early eighteenth centuries. During Elizabeth I's reign, tent stitch had begun to be used on embroidery furnishings to achieve a 'tapestry' effect. This stitch, properly worked, had a large proportion of silk or crewel wool on the underside which added greatly to its strength.

The Hope family asked us to design a wallhanging and together we agreed on a composite design (again the montage system of working) taken from the Devonshire Hunting Tapestries in the Victoria and Albert Museum. These marvellous panels have the distinctive vertical lines which were produced because the tapestries were worked sideways with

Right Sally King's medieval wallhanging. Ten years of inventive and exuberant stitchery make this panel a delight – look at the furry wildcats and layers of foliage

the 'cartoon' (from the word 'carton') of the original design placed behind the loom.

The Devonshire Hunting Tapestries are so called because they belonged to the Dukes of Devonshire and were hung at Chatsworth, and before that at Hardwick Hall; they have been at the Victoria and Albert Museum since 1957. There have been many rival opinions among tapestry historians of the origins of these pieces and it is most probable that they were woven in Arras in France in the fifteenth century. They show spectacular hunting and hawking scenes, and the lords and ladies who take the field are magnificently attired despite the wild nature of the forest. The designs are very strong and disregard all sense of proportion. There are ships and castles, ferocious bear hunts, romantic groups, men in turbans on dromedaries. The Devonshire Hunting Tapestries are like stepping into another world.

We decided to use 16-hole canvas, particularly because of the detail on the faces, and it was worked in crewel wool to give us as much scope as possible with both this fine detail and bigger stitchery. Depressingly, at that time the only canvas available in the right width was antique colour and this meant priming each section white before it was painted. We had to erect a small scaffold on which to work and life was altogether as uncomfortable as it could be, for such a gracious art. The stitchery was wonderful to work out, with its grand gestures of large expanses and textures. Evelyn Hope was fully absorbed for many years, and the result speaks for itself.

Far left The Hope Tapestry

Left Sally King working a chairseat based on a medieval theme

Sally King's wallhanging was specifically for a panelled dining room. The border and corner motifs picked out details of Minton china, which figured prominently in the room. The wallhanging took ten years to complete. During those years just about every feature of Sally's life changed. The tapestry travelled all over the world, and was shown by us under lock and key at a London exhibition. The original house with the panelled dining room has long gone, but the tapestry goes on—and on.

The decoration in the new dining room was created around the tapestry, not the other way round. Rather like a Van Gogh painting, the passion that went into every inch of this wallhanging seems to transcend the boundaries of the wool and canvas of which it was made. Sally does not know the meaning of any word except 'perfectionist' and we saw her once unpick the entire tree trunk because she found a preferable stitch. There is no question that the result was worth it. A lot of time goes into discussing and experimenting with the stitchery and we love it when one of our protegées takes off on her own.

The project for this section (spectacle case and bookmark) shows motifs immediately recognisable from the spectacular Cluny tapestries in Paris. Because these items are very fine and for practical reasons need to be as unlikely to catch as possible, we have worked them mostly in tent stitch. This has also been the clearest way to show the vertical look of the weave typical of such work.

The 'Lady with the Unicorn' series has appeared in so many reproductions, so many cards, tapestries, workboxes, that it was with a sense of yawning duty we visited the Cluny Museum in Paris. Reproductions leave you totally unprepared for the heart-stoppingness of the Cluny tapestries, hanging in their quietly lit womb. Five of the six panels are a fantasy of senses and are easily explained: Sight, Hearing, Smell, Touch, Taste. The sixth panel is enigmatic and had even been thought to belong to a different series, but it is now believed that the lady is renouncing all desire 'A mon seul desir'—which gives the six panels a moral significance. The lady stands on a dark-blue island set with flowering plants, birds and animals on a rich background of red, full of the characteristic mille-fleurs. Those involved in the series, the painter of the cartoons and the weavers, used all their ingenuity to produce a work which probably has more enchanting significance today than when it was created in the fifteenth century. In some places the weaving is crude, but the beauty of the panels is not lessened—on the contrary, for us it adds to their charm, because in general the details have great delicacy. The six pieces were brought to the public's attention by George Sand in 1847. It is known that they were commissioned by Jean le Viste, but their place of origin in the Low Countries—there are arguments for Bruges and Brussels—is still undetermined and the designer completely unidentified.

Having the same wonderful impact are the 'Hunts of the Unicorn', six similar pieces in the New York Metropolitan Museum's Cloisters. One does not expect to find such a wonderful evocation of medieval Europe so short a distance from the heart of Manhattan.

Left Lady with the Unicorn tapestry, from the Cluny Museum, Paris (*Reunion des musées nationaux*)

Right Some canvases on a medieval theme — the Cluny book open at the bottom of the page. *Inset* Spectacle case and bookmark using Cluny motifs

ready wit was often put to the test. On one occasion three *hetairæ* were presented to him for him
to make a choice : he took then all three, observ-
ing that it had been fatal even to Paris to make a
choice. On another occasion, in a dispute with
Æschines, who was becoming violent, he said,
"Let us give over : we have quarrelled, it is true
but I, as your senior, have a right to claim the
precedency in the reconciliation."

In old age he appears to have returned to
Cyrene, and there opened his school.

His philosophy, as Hegel remarks, takes its c...
from his personality. So individual is it,...
should have passed it over entirely, had it n...
a precursor of Epicureanism. Its rela...
Socrates is also important. Its rel...

In the only passage, we believe, in w...
stotle† mentions Aristippus, he speaks ...
Sophist. What does this mean? Wa...
the professor Sophists?—No. It me...
lieve, that he shared the opinion of ...
add the best of them — Scinus, the reas...
Aristippus over his house. While he was...
splendour of every part, even to the fl...
spat in his face. Scinus a furious...
claimed Aristippus, "there was no other p...
have spat with decency." One day, a...
Tyrant for a friend, he threw himse...
reproached for such want of dignity ...
fault if Dionysius has his ears in ...
asked the Tyrant for some money...
own that a philosopher had no...
give," replied Aristippus, "and...
once," Dionysius gave, "and...
have no need of money."...

* Several of his repartees are recorded...
† 'Met.,' iii. c. ii.

...ence. That he
...nt from Sextus
...ns ; such as that
...pressions on dif-
...we impose on these
...but do not express
...um of truth ; each
...essions ; none judge
...hist ; but, as the dis-
...d that the *criterion* of
...thin. He sought there,
...pt all physical specula-
...nd human comprehension,
...researches upon the moral
...Socratist. But, although he
...on from Socrates, yet his own
...ly turned him into by-paths
...ould have shunned. His was not
...eet. Logical deduction, which
...s pieces of his master, suited
...rs nor his disposition. He was
...t speculations. His tendency was
...ds the concrete. Hence,while Socrates
...g about The Good, Aristippus wished
...at it was ; and resolved it into Plea-
...was the pith and kernel of Socrates'
...stem, that Happiness was the aim and
...all men—the motive of all action ; men
...red because of erroneous notions of what
...ted Happiness. Thus the wise man alone
...that to endure an injury was better than to
...it ; he alone knew that immoderate gratifi-

* 'Adv. Math.,' vii. p. 173.

CLUNY BOOKMARK AND SPECTACLE CASE

Cluny Bookmark
Finished size of design: 2in × 9in (5 × 23cm)

Cluny Spectacle Case
Finished size of design: 4in × 7½in (10 × 19cm)
Tracings: page 180

MATERIALS

CLUNY BOOKMARK
Appleton's crewel wool

Blue	561	1 skein
Pale Green	641	1 skein
Grey Green	922	1 skein
Cream	881	1 skein
Custard	851	1 skein
Ochre	473	1 skein
Red	865	1 skein
Dark Green background	157	2 skeins

CLUNY SPECTACLE CASE

Blue	561	1 skein
Pale Green	641	1 skein
Grey Green	922	1 skein
Cream	881	1 skein
Custard	851	1 skein
Ochre	473	1 skein
Red	865	1 skein
Dark Green background	157	2 skeins

Note: if you are sewing both projects you will need only one skein of each colour and four skeins of background wool

White interlocked canvas, 18 holes to the inch.
Canvas size Cluny Bookmark: 12in × 5in (31 × 13cm)
Cluny Spectacle Case: 8in × 11in
(21 × 28 cm)
Size 22 needle
Ruler or tape measure
Masking tape for binding the canvas
Sharp scissors for cutting the canvas
Embroidery scissors
Sharp HB pencil or fine permanent marker in a suitable
colour
Eraser

HOW TO MARK THE CANVAS
Cut the canvas to size and tape the edges.

Trace the outline (page 180) onto the canvas following the thread where possible. Be sure to centre the tracing. If you are experienced at transferring designs it is only necessary to trace the thick lines onto the canvas—the finer lines are a guide to show where the colours change. If, however, you are not experienced, trace the fine lines on as well, perhaps in another colour.

HOW TO STITCH
Two strands are used throughout except for the stems of the flowers when one strand has been used.

Stitches used
 1 tent stitch
 2 split back stitch
 5 French knots
19 chain stitch

The stitch cards will show you how to do the stitches. The numbers on the drawing refer to the stitch card numbers. Refer to the colour picture and drawing to show you which colour goes where.

Begin by working the flowers and leaves in TENT stitch (1) and the centres of the flowers in FRENCH KNOTS (5). Leave the stems until the end. Then stitch the gold border at the top in horizontal CHAIN stitch (19) and TENT stitch (1). Fill in the background in TENT stitch (1). Do not pull too tightly as the canvas will show through. Finally, work the stems using one strand of crewel wool in SPLIT BACK stitch (2).

The motifs on the tracings could be enlarged and the design worked on larger canvas for a cushion or a stool. For practical reasons these items are worked mainly in TENT stitch with a little stitchery for added interest.

MAKING UP INSTRUCTIONS
After you have finished stitching the spectacle case/bookmark, it may be necessary to stretch the design back to shape. Then make up into a spectacle case, or bookmark (see Chapter 15).

881   473   561   922

851   865   641   157

CHAPTER 8
NEEDLEPOINT FROM ART

The Royal Academy, founded in 1768, is the oldest, and possibly the liveliest, art institution in Great Britain. In the words of Sir Hugh Casson, a past President, 'It is difficult to imagine anyone today having the temerity, or indeed the vision, to invent so remarkable an institution as the Royal Academy, guided not by a bureaucracy but practising artists of national stature.'

Following the success of the British Museum Collection, Selena Fellows of the Royal Academy approached us to collaborate with Frederick Gore on a needlepoint design for the Summer Exhibition in 1981. A design for the Great Japan Exhibition followed, based on fans from a silk robe from the late Edo period. Later, we designed two pictures for the Venice Exhibition. The idea began to develop for a series of needlepoint designs to revive the traditional marriage between artist and craftsman. Selena orchestrated the 'auditioning' of Royal Academicians whose work we felt would best lend itself to our hopefully-not-too-unsympathetic medium. We finally decided on four: Bernard Dunstan, Leonard Rosoman, Philip Sutton and Edward Wolfe. The project was full of wonderful incidents and involved six months of intensive battle with the limitations of yarn and canvas. We had always felt needlepoint reproductions of fine art to be crude and embarrassing insults to the painters and were determined not to be added to the guilty list.

Two of the artists painted pictures especially for us. We loved Leonard Rosoman's print of a room seen from outside, with the trees behind reflected on the glass. He did a version of this, creating a frame of brickwork, the reflections of trees and trellis in the window making semi-abstract patterns, the pianist inside the room suspended in an inside-out garden. He writes, 'For some years I have been interested in various forms of the double image. This design of a window in my own house is built on the "marriage" of two views—looking through the lower panes of glass I see a fragmented arrangement of certain objects inside the room, a girl sitting at a piano, flowers in vases, etc. As I raise my eyes upwards, the reflection of what is in the garden behind me becomes dominant—a trellis, various plants and branches silhouetted against the sky. These two separate images melt into each other and create an entirely new one which is mysteriously trapped in the box-like shape of the window itself. The stylised brickwork of the border emphasises this isolation and I get the feeling that I'm looking at something secret and exciting.'

Edward Wolfe was the last surviving member of the Bloomsbury Set. He has been described as 'a lyrical painter with a sensuality rare in England . . . but he is tough and holds, from old experience, a pack of cards in store, dealing out his yellows, vermilions, curious hot pinks and illumined blues with the confidence of a man who trusts his vision.'

In the painting we chose, 'Still Life with Flowers', the mask on the mirrored table is a reminder of his interest in the theatre, and the box behind is decorated in Omega Workshop style. We used fourteen colours of wool and fourteen coton perlé and feel the interaction of yarn and stitchery in this design reflects so well his love of vitality and colour. Even the table where we were entertained for lunch by him, was a mélange of painted and antique china, superb fruits—a marvellous still life of a table, overhanging the Thames and wharfs. He died soon after the project was undertaken and we are privileged to use his work for the collection.

Manet's 'Olympia' inspired Philip Sutton to produce his version in the form of a woodblock print. We liked the simplicity of it, and the way in

Right Still Life with Flowers (Edward Wolfe), the Window Image (Leonard Rosoman) and, in the background, Manet Lady (Philip Sutton).

The Royal Academy Collection, needlepoint designs reviving the traditional marriage between artist and craftsman

which crewel wool could imitate the jagged linear quality of the print. It was a total departure from anything we had ever attempted.

With Bernard Dunstan there was no question of what we wanted—the definitive Dunstan. A nude, early Italian light, wafting curtaining, patterned walls. He writes, 'Hotel rooms become my studio when we are abroad. They are all the same, yet all different, and I never get tired of the subtle variations of light and colour. Volterra is an ideal town for the painter, a hill town of just the right size, full of subjects both in the town and in the magnificent country around. But my subject here is one that I paint over and over again with enjoyment and a sense of discovery, a nude on a bed with Italian light through shutters or curtains.' He produced an exquisite pastel of such subtlety and serenity that he said himself, 'You know this is impossible—why are you doing it?' The answer is in the question. To put floating, gentle, pastel nuances into a medium that has solid edges, and severe limitations, to try to be as faithful as possible to the original, losing none of the feeling—yes, the reasoning has to be questioned. First, there was the desire to do justice to such beautiful work, for his work is truly beautiful, and to compensate all those crude Fragonard girls and Renoir women. Secondly, to produce a kit for other people to work, with a feasible number of printed colours and yarns, with instructions simple enough to be followed. Finally, because it was 'impossible'! So, perversity was the reason—to make it work, to see how far we could stretch the boundaries of needlepoint.

The picture was first broken down into a number of colours and with those strangling restrictions, copied onto canvas. The artist then corrected it himself on the same canvas. We then produced a new canvas incorporating those corrections in workable terms and the process was repeated. Eventually we arrived at a needlepoint canvas acceptable to us all. The main problem then began.

To paint with wool as a one-only piece, to improvise and suggest with splashes of colour, with unlimited yarns, to create flashes of light, tiny rainbow points, would have been an indulgent delight. The purpose of this was different. Sitting hour after hour to make that body right, limiting the colours, to be logically repeatable, blending those

Right Morning Volterra, from the Royal Academy Collection. It is shown with the pastel by Bernard Dunstan which inspired it, and an intermediate 'working' canvas with the artist's corrections and wool experiments

few colours to create other tones—knowing there *had* to be a way of achieving it—that was a challenge—a fascinating challenge.

This particular picture illustrates perfectly the versatility of crewel wool. Blending the strands of colour on the figure and in the shadows achieves the merging of shades. Single strands of wool have been used for the curtains to give the diaphanous look we wanted, a single strand for the suggestion of the handrail on the balcony. The wallpaper is worked in blocks of unblended colour to give solidity—and this is one design where colours of a similar tonal value have been used together—the pink, green and brown of the wallpaper work excellently because they are all the same mid-tone. The lighter cream and brighter blue create a good contrast. Equally, on the figure—green, mauve and brown do not sound a promising recipe for successful flesh tints and yet they work beautifully because of their similar tonal value.

'Morning, Volterra' was probably the most laboured-over kit we have produced. With a press launch organised at the Academy, and still refusing to compromise on tiny details of the stitching—teeth became clenched, temperaments less sunny. One thread worked left or right can make a difference—with paint you can correct with a slight gesture, in needlepoint this means unpicking, securing threads, starting a new thread . . . and we are talking here of minuscule changes. Nights hunched over the canvas, with the late night radio phone-ins to help stay awake, then somehow, one night, it was right, and it was finished. As with anything creative—from painting to cooking—an instinct says, 'That's it, not another stitch, stroke, leaf, grain.' Our state-of-the-art , equivalently-perfectionist framer, Michael Gentry, framed this last of the four pictures overnight, and with a nail biting photo-finish, everything was done.

The designs are certainly among the best kits we have produced because the instructions enable anybody to interpret fine art into needlepoint.

MONET

And then there is Monet, the impossible-to-translate Monet. As with the old Chinese attitude to art, one can only hope to capture the essence rather than depict it accurately. To be rigidly bound by his power and colours was not our intention; but we wanted to convey his love for what he was touched by. The starting point for the chair was a painting he did of his garden at Giverny in 1910, a marvellous impression of bowers and blooms. To visit Giverny and not be moved by the vision and achievement of Monet is hard to imagine. We have both, through changing seasons, been overwhelmed by the wisterias and azaleas and the uncontainable world of the water lilies. This chair has become a homage to Monet and provides beautiful memories of dozens of hours, spent cross-legged on the floor, working with a friend who cared equally about the project. The design was worked on 7-hole canvas using four or five strands of crewel wool, which was mixed as paint would be, referring continually to the painting to suggest the nuances that are there. Threading up each needle of mixed tones probably took longer than sewing each length of wool. We used an encroaching long and short stitch worked at an angle of 45 degrees to give best coverage and a feeling of movement.

The design was painted loosely onto the canvas in oils, with colours suggested only approximately. Right up to the end the colour mixing was as improvised and experimental as at the beginning (though surer and quicker) and it was constantly surprising how a single thread on a piece that size could distract the eye when it was unharmonious. Again, as with 'Morning, Volterra', the shades can be mixed in one 'needleful' but the tones must be similar.

'Monet Poppies', is inspired by a picture painted at Argenteuil in 1873. We have taken a small section of what we consider 'the heart of the painting' and, with stitchery, imitated the painterly aspects of Monet's work. The continuous mosaic on the trees gives an effect of contrast and movement, and an encroaching long and short stitch for the field gives the feeling of a breeze moving through the grass. Working the satin for the poppies in this same direction keeps the eye moving around the picture, coming only to rest on the model's parasol, with its straight lines, that 'grounds' the picture.

| *Right* The Monet chair

THE VENETIAN DESIGNS

Spending a lot of time in a place during formative years can leave permanently echoing images in the mind and heart. We have both spent a lot of time in Venice, together and separately, so as a needlepoint source it was irresistible.

The 'Pierrot' and 'Columbine' were the first designs to have a Venetian watery theme, and the elements we always associate with the city—a suggestion of carnival, fantasy, mystery, the mandolin and masks. The buildings and water are indivisible; one dissolves into the other. The needle moves from the fluid strokes of the sky, to stone, then to water with the ease of an eye unable to distinguish where the line is drawn.

The small Venetian pair were commissioned by the Royal Academy for their Venice Exhibition, and we loved them both so much that later, and on a larger scale, we elaborated on the bridges and carnival motifs, using rich silks combined with wool.

Right These Venetian themes – the Pierrot and Columbine, the fantasy of Venetian architecture, and echoes of carnival – have made a fascinating needlepoint inter-pretation

MONET'S POPPIES

Finished size of design: 7in × 9in (18 × 23cm)
Tracing: page 184

MATERIALS
Appleton's crewel wool

A	Pale Green	874	1 skein
B	Grey Green	641	2 skeins
C	Mid Grey Green	155	1 skein
D	Dark Grey Green	157	1 skein
E	Grass Green	353	1 skein
F	Olive Green	343	1 skein
G	Bright Green	831	1 skein
H	Honey	882	1 skein
J	Pale Blue	876	2 skeins
K	Mid Blue	561	1 skein
L	Airforce Blue	923	1 skein
M	Dull Mauve	931	1 skein
N	Brown	122	1 skein
O	Charcoal	998	1 skein

Anchor stranded cotton

P	Orange	0333	1 skein
R	Red	0339	1 skein
S	Terracotta	0337	1 skein

White interlocked canvas or antique mono deluxe canvas, 18 holes to the inch
Canvas size: 11in × 13in (28 × 33cm)
Size 22 needle
Ruler or tape measure
Masking tape for binding the canvas
Sharp scissors for cutting the canvas
Embroidery scissors
Sharp HB pencil or fine permanent marker in a suitable
    colour, and eraser

HOW TO MARK THE CANVAS
Cut the canvas to size and tape the edges.

Trace the design (page 184) onto the canvas in the centre. The fine lines denote the change in shades of wool and can be put on freehand if you are confident. Otherwise trace them through. Using a marker in a different colour may be helpful. The areas filled with fine diagonal lines show where the poppies are and the direction they are sewn in. The black areas are to be sewn in charcoal wool.

HOW TO STITCH
Six strands of stranded cotton (the whole thread) are used on the poppies and on the band of the child's hat.

Two strands of crewel wool have been used everywhere else with the exception of the grass when one strand is used and on the umbrella when three strands have been used.

Stitches used
  1 tent stitch
  2 back stitch
  3 satin stitch
  4 diagonal long and short stitch (encroaching)
  12 upright cross stitch
  17 continuous mosaic stitch

Before beginning to stitch, it is advisable to write the colour code on the label of the wool, or you could thread a piece of wool at the side of the canvas and write the code names against it, but use a permanent marker!

The stitch cards will show you how to do the stitches. The numbers refer to the stitch cards. The letters (overleaf) refer to the colours.

Begin by sewing the figures. Work their faces in TENT stitch (1) in the opposite direction from the card; this is to follow the jaw line. The lady's dress is in CONTINUOUS MOSAIC stitch (17). The umbrella is in vertical SATIN stitch (3), in three strands of wool edged in pale green BACK stitch (2), the handle is in diagonal SATIN stitch (3). The child's dress is in UPRIGHT CROSS stitch (12) and his arm is in TENT stitch (1). The hats and hair are in SATIN stitch (3). Stitch the trees in CONTINUOUS MOSAIC stitch (17) and the sky in TENT stitch (1).

The grass has been worked diagonally at a 45 degree angle in encroaching LONG AND SHORT stitch (4) using one thread of crewel wool. Try to keep the stitch to a similar length and sew along the same diagonal angle, so that the grass looks as if it is blowing in the breeze. If any white canvas shows through, sew extra filling-in stitches.

Finally stitch the poppies at the same diagonal angle in SATIN stitch (3) in stranded cotton.

MAKING UP INSTRUCTIONS
After the design has been sewn, it may be necessary to stretch it back to shape (Chapter 15). You may prefer to take your work to a professional framer in which case, they will stretch it for you.

MONET'S POPPIES

CHAPTER 9
VICTORIANA

Above Victorian Scraps

Overleaf A Victorian setting, with richly textured needlepoint, flowers and decoration to excess, against sombre wood

As a contrast to light trellis and pastels, tastes generally are reverting to traditional style and a heavier Victorian look, with richer colouring and patterning. We find ourselves strongly influenced by pieces of antique beadwork and Berlin work embroidery, as anyone who visits The Old Mill House will know. For such an old art as needlework, we try to refer to the origins of what we are expressing, wanting the pieces to have a beauty that lasts. Needlework, by its nature, is not 'disposable'.

In Victorian days the more leisured lady produced an abundance of embroidery for her home. Every possible item in the overcrowded rooms would be covered with some form of needlework—often Berlin work which, as its name implies, had its origins in Berlin. This work consisted of a series of designs printed onto squared paper and easily interpreted by the amateur onto squared canvas. At first these designs were worked in soft wool, but later beads were added. Sometimes the designers used contemporary artists' work as their source material—Landseer's animals or the well known floral designs of the period, which often became exaggerated and larger than life. The newly produced aniline dyestuffs also offered the embroiderer a whole range of exciting new colours: magenta, pinks, purples, etc. Berlin work often incorporated different stitches, such as Turkey work (a furry stitch), giving an extra dimension to the otherwise flat effect.

At the same time there was a great enthusiasm for couching and braiding; cross-stitch pictures of romanticised medieval subjects with scenes of chivalry and castle ruins; and Japanese screens crowded with cranes and bamboo. The Victorians loved what they called Fancy Work. Fancy Work covered a multitude of different techniques, including embroidery in ribbons and coloured gauzes, fish-scale embroidery using pierced dried fish scales as a 'decorative' feature. William Morris was probably the antidote to the Fancy Work craze, preferring an integrity of design and simplicity of stitches. Eventually he, too, produced ready drawn designs, with specially dyed threads (not aniline dyes, for he is said to have hated the colours they produced) for sale to the amateur—the forerunner of the needlepoint kit.

Recently, we have begun using the busy clusters and rich colours of the flowers the Victorians loved so much, the satisfyingly fat roses, funereal lilies and an organised extravagant formality. Again, we wanted to give these designs the essence, the impression of the Victorian themes and the whole look benefits from being seen 'en masse', pattern on pattern—almost impossible to overdo. Use cushions to excess, just keep piling them on!

We have been commissioned to paint canvases for many special chairs and stools. Inspired by beaded Victorian bell pulls, wallhangings, upholstery, teapot stands, we particularly love the subtle grey-and-mauve combinations often seen in beadwork. The designs are now completing a cycle—as you can see on the right of the picture on page 113, we are using full-blown Victorian roses and are reverting to a more typically Glorafilia pastel look.

The round design chosen for the project is shown as a stool and also as a round cushion, with either charcoal or honey background. The design typifies for us the opulence of the Victorian floral look. You can, of course, continue to work it into a square and enlarge it to fit a particular stool or seat.

The 'Fruit Pincushion' (page 120) demonstrates the different applications an exciting design can inspire. The original tiny framed Victorian picture was worked very loosely in long and short stitches in wool and metal threads, as if by a very unsteady and quivering hand. There is something so alive about the design, even with its sombre colours, so much movement through the stitchery. We worked the footstool first on a large scale and then a miniature full of shaded shapes.

The two small cushions on the right of the fruit picture were inspired by Victorian tiles. (London's museums and street markets, such as Portobello Road, are particularly rich in good examples.) They are a wonderful design source because their composition is usually superb—as, for instance, where large lilies are successfully coaxed into the discipline of a square-shaped tile.

VICTORIAN CIRCLE

Finished size of design: 11in (28cm) diameter

MATERIALS
Appleton's tapestry wool

Very Pale Peach	881	¼ hank (18 × 30in/75cm lengths)
Peach	705	¼ hank (18 × 30in/75cm lengths)
Mushroom	203	¼ hank (18 × 30in/75cm lengths)
Rose Pink	222	½ hank (36 × 30in/75cm lengths)
Dark Rose Pink	225	¼ hank (18 × 30in/75cm lengths)
Lime Green	331	¾ hank (54 × 30in/75cm lengths)
Pale Green	641	¼ hank (18 × 30in/75cm lengths)
Dark Green	644	¼ hank (18 × 30in/75cm lengths)
Blue	886	⅛ hank (9 × 30in/75cm lengths)
Lilac	712	⅛ hank (9 × 30in/75cm lengths)
Purple	103	⅛ hank (9 × 30in/75cm lengths)

Choice of backgrounds

Honey	882	1¼ hanks (90 × 30in/75cm lengths)
or Charcoal	998	1¼ hanks (90 × 30in/75cm lengths)

White mono deluxe canvas, 14 holes to the inch
Size of canvas: 15in × 15in (38cm)
Size 20 needle
Compass
Ruler or tape measure
Masking tape for binding the canvas
Sharp scissors for cutting the canvas
Embroidery scissors
Sharp HB pencil or fine permanent marker in a suitable colour
Eraser

HOW TO MARK THE CANVAS

Cut the canvas to size and bind the edges with masking tape. If you plan to make this design into a circular shape it may be easier to draw a circle onto the canvas with the compass before beginning to stitch. The hole that the compass point goes in will be the centre of the design.

See General Information for useful hints on how to work from a colour chart.

HOW TO STITCH

The whole thread is used throughout.

Stitches used

For a traditional finish the design can be worked in TENT stitch (1). Alternatively, it can be worked using stitchery as we have shown but this is more complicated.

1 tent stitch
3 satin stitch
4 long and short stitch
5 French knots
13 brick stitch over two threads

The stitch cards (see page 13) will show you how to do the stitches. The numbers on the outline drawing refer to the numbers on the stitch cards. Refer to the colour picture and especially to the black cushion for the position and direction of the stitches. It is quite complicated to do stitchery from a chart (see page 118)—bear this in mind before beginning this project.

Begin to sew either at the centre or at the top of the design.

The BRICK stitch (13) is all horizontal and worked over two threads of canvas. The roses and parrot tulips are all worked in TENT stitch (1). The buds are in BRICK stitch (13) and most of the leaves are also in BRICK stitch (13); the smaller ones are in SATIN stitch (3) and TENT stitch (1). The blue flowers are sewn in LONG AND SHORT stitch (4), radiating out from the centre and the centres are in TENT stitch (1) and FRENCH KNOTS (5). The background is worked in TENT stitch (1) in honey or charcoal.

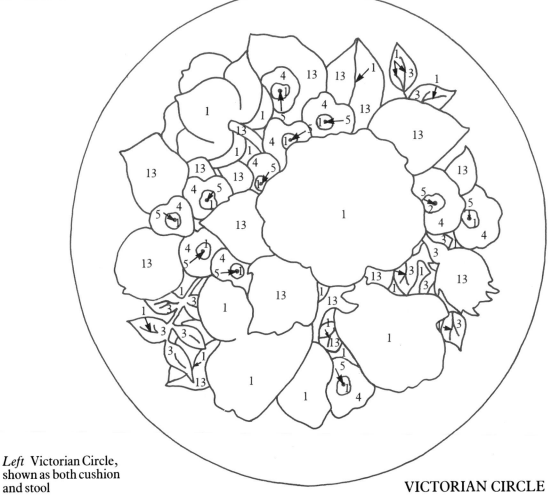

Left Victorian Circle, shown as both cushion and stool

VICTORIAN CIRCLE

This is a wonderfully rich and adaptable design and we have used this pattern for chair seats, bell pulls, stools and rugs. Worked on 22-canvas in stranded cotton or crewel wool it would make a wonderful miniature petit point design.

MAKING UP INSTRUCTIONS
After sewing the design stretch back into shape (see Chapter 15) and then make into a stool or cushion (also Chapter 15).

VICTORIAN CIRCLE

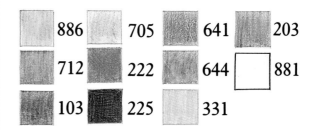

886	705	641	203
712	222	644	881
103	225	331	

FRUIT PINCUSHION

Finished size of design: 5¼in square (13cm)
Tracing: page 178

MATERIALS
Appleton's crewel wool

DM	Dark Mauve (background)	934	2 skeins
M	Mauve	932	1 skein
L	Lilac	601	1 skein
H	Heather	883	1 skein
N	Navy Blue	747	1 skein
R	Royal Blue	745	1 skein
B	Pale Blue	741	1 skein
T	Terracotta	204	1 skein
PT	Pale Terracotta	202	1 skein
P	Pink	751	1 skein
F	Flesh	877	1 skein
C	Cinnamon	696	1 skein
G	Gold	694	1 skein
HO	Honey	691	1 skein
O	Olive Green	242	1 skein
J	Jacobean Green	403	1 skein
PG	Pale Green	341	1 skein
MG	Mid Green	292	1 skein

White interlocked canvas, 18 holes to the inch
Canvas size: 9in × 9in (23 × 23cm)
Size 22 needle
Masking tape for binding the canvas
Ruler or tape measure
Sharp scissors for cutting the canvas
Embroidery scissors
Sharp HB pencil or fine permanent marker in a
 suitable colour
Eraser

HOW TO MARK THE CANVAS
Cut the canvas to size and tape the edges. Trace the design (page 178) onto the centre of the canvas. The thick lines are the outline of the fruit and leaves. The fine lines are to show a change in the shade of wool. It is only necessary to trace the outer edges of the fruit (the thick lines) onto the canvas; if you are confident, copy the fine lines freehand, in another colour. Otherwise, trace these afterwards. Draw a line around the design on the thread of the canvas.

The black background on the tracing is the dark mauve background (934).

HOW TO STITCH
Two strands of wool are used throughout.

Stitches used
 1 tent stitch
 2 split back stitch
 3 satin stitch
 4 long and short stitch
 5 French knots
 22 long legged cross stitch

The stitch cards will show you how to do the stitches. The numbers refer to the numbers on the stitch cards. The letters on the diagram overleaf refer to the colours. Refer to the colour picture and the red arrows to show you the direction of the long and short stitches.

 The fruit has been worked in LONG AND SHORT stitch (4) with the exception of the grapes and blueberries, which are in diagonal SATIN stitch (3).

119

The leaves are also in LONG AND SHORT stitch (4). All the outlining and the stalks have been stitched in dark mauve SPLIT BACK stitch (DM2). The pomegranate seeds are pink FRENCH KNOTS (P5). The background areas filled in with black, are worked in dark mauve TENT stitch (DM1). The design is surrounded by LONG LEGGED CROSS stitch in dark mauve (DM22).

This design could be enlarged and sewn on 14- or 10-canvas, using tapestry wool. It would make a wonderful stool or cushion. We have also adapted the design for our beautiful antique stool—just enlarge the tracing and repeat the pattern.

MAKING UP INSTRUCTIONS

After the design has been sewn, it may be necessary to stretch it back to shape (see Chapter 15). Make it into a pincushion, with tassels (again see Chapter 15), or take it to a framer who will make it into a charming miniature.

Left The Fruit Theme – luscious large or small.

FRUIT PINCUSHION

CHAPTER 10
PERFECT PETS
AND
FAMILY
HEIRLOOMS

We have asked ourselves why we don't sit with our feet up and do needlepoint, but we don't get very intelligent replies. Apart from yoga, meditation, reading, it has to be one of the most serene things to do (don't lose your needles though, that can create a severe lack of serenity). Oh, we begin prototype canvases, experiment with stitchery and colourings, correct canvases and finish them off. Once in a very rare while, there will be something like the

Giverny chair, but generally we never have the satisfaction of beginning and ending a piece of needlepoint. Except—we do stitch dolls.

The intention was to do them for our children for birthdays and Christmasses—thus by the time they all came of age there would be great armies of much-loved heirlooms to hand on to future generations. In practice it didn't always work out that way and so our children quite often have been

Needlepoint dolls and animals will hopefully be treasured long after a shop-bought doll would have been discarded.

Even after many years of 'loving', a needlepoint doll will still have charm and character

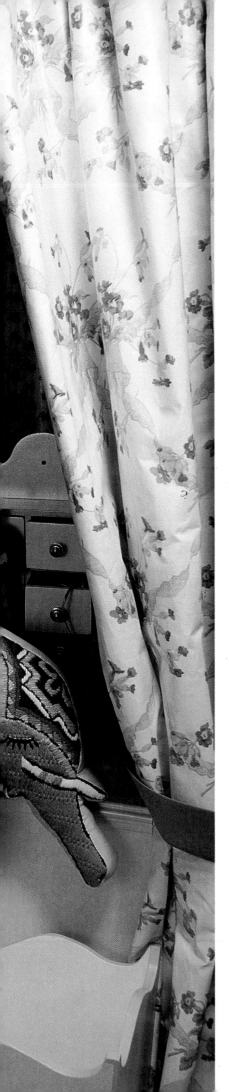

deprived. At different times we have both sat up half the night to complete an unfinished face or leg for the next morning; Jennifer once frantically having to start from scratch when she left an almost completed clown on a TWA flight.

The dolls are a delight to make, because the giving and receiving is so nice to anticipate. They usually don't take too long and lots of short cuts can be taken with the stitches. If the fate of the doll you make is that it will be loved and chewed beyond recognition by a small child, console yourself with how charming we now find antique dolls and teddies—threadbare, blinded, but full of character. Dolls in the relevant school uniform are always a good idea, with the right colour hair and any other personal characteristics. Tamsin had a 'robin' fetish, which she has never outgrown. Your particular favourite child may love monkeys, or rabbits—the doll can be as 'custom built' and as personal as you can make it.

The Perfect Pets are so called for obvious reasons. They look terrific on chair, floor or dresser, sitting on top of the stairs, high on a bookshelf, grouped on a sofa or bed. And . . . they require no maintenance! Again, they can be completed quite quickly—we have a chart for the 'Silver Tabby' or substitute your own colours.

If you plan to work a known (or remembered) favourite animal, make sure you capture his expression from the shape of mouth, eyes and the way the body is held. Photocopy and enlarge a photograph, mark the relevant patches in colour, or outline, then trace through onto canvas, match wools and begin.

Far left Alison among the family heirlooms

Decide carefully on the size—a lifesized Yorkie is one thing, a lifesize Great Dane quite another. As a rule, animals do not look good larger than life. We feel that pets look best in tent stitch—although the whiskers should be worked in split back stitch to give unbroken lines. This has a more traditional look, and animals in needlepoint have been around a long time.

Who could forget the pictures of the Duchess of Windsor's pugs, lined up at the end of the bed. As each pet died she had it replicated as a cushion, stuffed and propped up next to its brother. A little ghoulish, in fact, not a million miles away from poor Norman Bates's mother in *Psycho*. So we tend to make our pets decorative rather than memorial!

As cushions, they are quite comfortable to lean against, nice solid blocks of stuffing. An extension of this is the shaped cushion. In a group of cushions (most things are better grouped than alone, with the exception of pugs), the addition of a shape among the conventional square, round or oblong, can be very pleasing. They are intended to be informal and fun and look particularly good in a conservatory.

The first needlepoint editorial offer we did for the British newspaper, *The Sunday Times*, in 1978 was of a shaped cushion, a small basket of flowers. It seems strange to us now that we chose something unusual, when in those days there was a dearth of *anything* interesting in needlepoint. Tastes, public expectations and demands, have thankfully changed dramatically over these years and people are no longer content to do what the Viennese do, or what their grandmothers did—we are happy to be among those who are making the changes.

Far right Silver Tabby Cat shown with Black and White Cat and two Ginger Cats!

Right Cyclamen and Tulip Basket shaped cushions

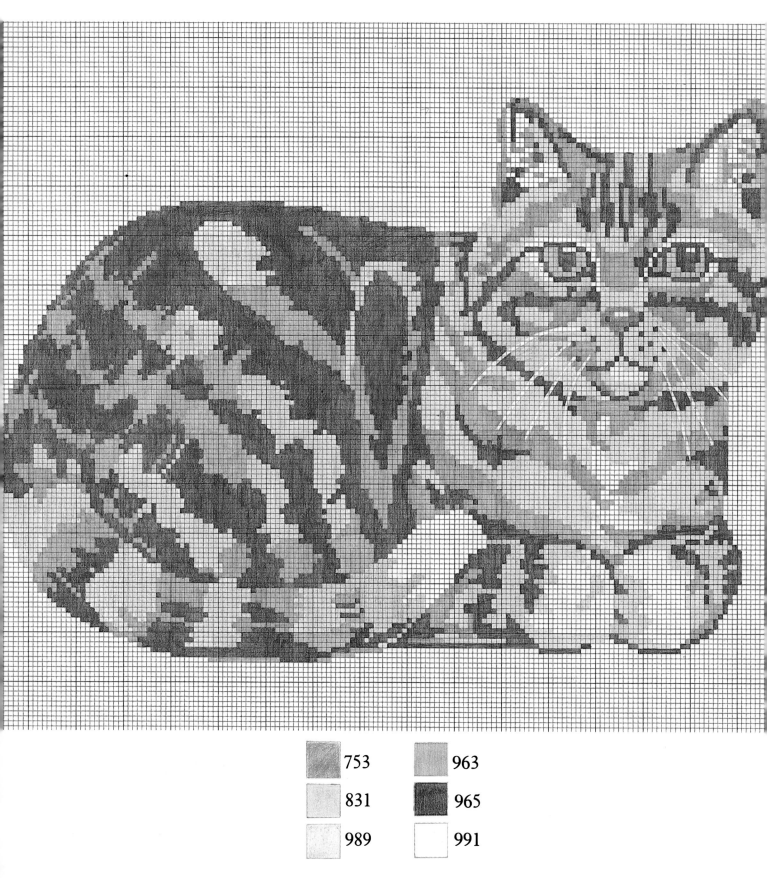

	753		963
	831		965
	989		991

SILVER TABBY CAT

SILVER TABBY CAT

Finished size of design: 12in × 9in (30 × 23cm)

MATERIALS
Appleton's tapestry wool

White	991 ¼ hank	(18 × 30in/75cm lengths)
Green	831 –	(3 × 30in/75cm lengths)
Pink	753 –	(3 × 30in/75cm lengths)
Pale Grey	989 ¾ hank	(54 × 30in/75cm lengths)
Mid Grey	963 ¾ hank	(54 × 30in/75cm lengths)
Dark Grey	965 1 hank	(72 × 30in/75cm lengths)

White mono deluxe canvas, 14 holes to the inch
Size of canvas: 16in × 13in (41 × 33cm)
Size 20 needle
Masking tape to bind the edge of the canvas
Sharp scissors for cutting the canvas
Embroidery scissors

THE CANVAS
The canvas does not have to be marked out, just follow the colour chart. See General Information for useful hints on how to work from a colour chart before beginning to stitch.

HOW TO STITCH
The whole thread is used throughout.

Stitches used
1 tent stitch
2 split back stitch

Cut the canvas to size and bind the edges. The stitch cards will show you how to do the stitches. Begin in any area you wish. It may be easier to start at the top right hand corner and work in horizontal bands of colour. The cat has been worked in TENT stitch (1) throughout with the exception of the whiskers which are in white SPLIT BACK stitch (2). Work these last.

MAKING UP INSTRUCTIONS
Stretch the design back into shape (see Chapter 15) and make up into a shaped cushion (see Chapter 15 also). Alternatively, you can sew the background to make an oblong cushion or picture, or weight the base of the cushion down with beans for a doorstop.

CHAPTER 11
RIBBONS
AND
BOWS

The insurance company trouble-shooter jetting to an exacting international assignment opens his executive brief case—and takes out his tapestry. He is oblivious to the wary stares of his fellow passengers, and the needlepoint provides a few blissful hours away from the high stress of big business. Robin Grey, who stitched some of our early samples, began needlepoint in this way and meeting him dispelled any thoughts we may have had, in those early days, that needlepoint was a genteel occupation for elderly ladies by the fireside.

Attitudes have changed and now more men than ever are needlepointing our kits. Rugs are worked by men and women, sometimes together, and certainly the British Museum Collection opened up an interest for many people who would never have touched the hearts and flowers generally available.

However, on one design area we are unashamedly feminine: ribbons and bows. The middle of the eighteenth century saw a development in embroidery design, from the heavy baroque floral motifs of the late sixteenth century to a lighter effect, sometimes incorporating ribbons into flower sprays, thus separating and lightening the whole look. Since then the ribbon motif has been used extensively.

Our shelves of wools and cottons, like tumbling rainbows, remind us of those old haberdashery shops, now almost extinct, where rows of mouth-watering ribbons and braids vied for attention. A recent Glorafilia catalogue had thirty designs in it with ribbons and bows—delicate, fine, bold, bright, large, billowing, on rugs, embroideries, pictures, cushions, doorstops, firescreens. Even the fabric we printed for our accessories has tiny lovers knots all over it. We have fat, contoured bows with short tails, and silky, narrow bows with long, flowing streamers. The natural empathy between ribbons and needlework means that the stitches can be persuaded into lovely lyrical shapes. We love to use the ribbon device, in linking motifs, in creating borders. With the change of a colour, movement can be suggested or shadows invented.

If you are drawing your own ribbon, the best way is to put a ribbon down in front of you, either coaxing it a little into the shape you want, or letting it fall and make its own natural rhythm (which will undoubtedly be better than anything contrived).

As long as we use flowers as a theme, we shall continue to use ribbons and bows—with what else can a posy be tied or a single flower clasped so deliciously?

The ribbon motif is something we love, and wherever we use needlepoint, we have used bows, from discreet lovers knots to flamboyant wallhangings

A perfect room for some
of our needlepoint bows –
the carpet and desk are
both 'beribboned'

461
741
744
463
464
471
991

RIBBON DOORSTOP

Finished brick: 9in × 4in × 2¾in (23 × 10 × 7cm)

MATERIALS
Appleton's tapestry wool

White	991	1½ hanks (108 × 30in/75cm lengths)
Yellow	471	¾ hank (54 × 30in/75cm lengths)
Pale Blue	461	¼ hank (18 × 30in/75cm lengths)
China Blue	741	½ hank (36 × 30in/75cm lengths)
Wedgewood Blue	744	½ hank (36 × 30in/75cm lengths)
Cornflower Blue	463	⅓ hank (24 × 30in/75cm lengths)
Royal Blue	464	½ hank (36 × 30in/75cm lengths)

White mono deluxe canvas, 14 holes to the inch
Size of canvas: 18in × 13in (46 × 33cm)
Size 20 needle
Masking tape for binding the canvas
Sharp scissors for cutting the canvas
Embroidery scissors
Tape measure or ruler

THE CANVAS
The canvas does not have to be marked out, just follow the colour chart. See General Information for useful hints on working from a colour chart before beginning to stitch.

HOW TO STITCH
The whole thread is used throughout. The whole design is worked in TENT stitch (1).

Cut the canvas to size and tape the edges. The stitch card will show you how to do the stitch. Begin in any area you wish. It may be easier to start at the top part of the ribbon and work horizontally in bands of colour. Stitch the ribbon first, followed by the 'spots' and finally the background. The background is sewn in white wool.

The blue corner marks are only meant as a guide. It is not necessary to sew the corner areas in blue just continue in white to the marks. The finished shape should look like Diagram 1.

If you want to make an oblong cushion from the design, simply continue working the background to the ribbon edges and put in more yellow 'spots'.

MAKING UP INSTRUCTIONS
Stretch the design back into shape and make up into a doorstop, see Chapter 15.

DIAGRAM 1

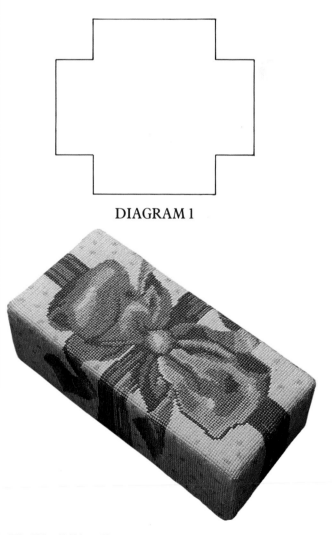

| The Blue Ribbon Doorstop

135

CHAPTER 12
APPLIQUÉ

The word *appliqué* comes from the Latin *applicare* meaning to fold or to fasten together. This technique was originally used to strengthen fabric, but soon other possibilities were discovered as it proved to be a far quicker form of decoration than any other. During the nineteenth century, when the East India Company supplied households with highly ornate cotton bedcovers, the thrifty house-wife soon discovered that, once the cover came to the end of its life, it could be cut up and used to decorate other articles. Our homes are full of memories as we recycle and change the use of beautiful fabrics. An oriental robe becomes cushions; teacosies become pictures; an antique silk shirt now covers a chair, and a tablecloth is adorned with tiny cuttings from a Byzantine print.

Appliqué is a superb way of creating a dramatic cushion with less work than stitching a whole canvas. The subject should have a shape that is easily cut round; it can either have a curved or jagged edge. Obviously, the softer the outside shape is, the easier it is to turn in the canvas and keep the design smooth. The peony design shown on the bamboo chair (overleaf) is perfect for appliqué—the edge has an interesting shape and yet it is easy to apply, the design radiates out from the centre like a sunburst and looks very dramatic.

Design elements can be taken from fabric and supplemented with other motifs to give variety, and form an interesting group. As with most cushions—unless something very special—they look better en masse, so don't be afraid to 'pile them high'! Repetition enhances the whole look. Furniture in itself is static, but cushions bring softness and movement in the most natural way and appliqués can make a beautiful and interesting feature with relatively little effort.

Indeed, there was relatively little effort involved for the owner of the appliqués shown by the fire. The client who commissioned them to match her fabric was too involved making beautiful pottery to work the designs herself, so we stitched them for her!

The appliqué tulips on the cushion on the rocking chair (page 143) have also been used to upholster the chair effectively. In this case, of

| *Right* Appliqué cushions

course, they have not been appliquéd, but the background has been fully worked. In order to do this, trace the two tulips, juxtaposing them however you like until they please you. For a seat cover it would be best to work on tracing paper; plan where the flowers are to go with a pencil, then trace through the shapes of the flowers, turning them so that they do not repeat the direction of the flower alongside. Stand back and look at the general positioning, or try it on the seat to see how near the flowers can come to the edge, and finally, when satisfied, trace strongly in felt pen over the pencil lines, and then trace through onto the canvas.

Left Three appliqués — one echoing the rose on the fabric, the others using favourite subjects in the same colours

Right Peony Appliqué

VIOLET APPLIQUÉ

Finished size of design: 7in × 7in (18 × 18cm)
Tracing: page 185

MATERIALS
Anchor stranded cotton

White	01	1 skein
Mauve	96	1 skein
Pale Violet	108	1 skein
Mid Violet	109	1 skein
Purple	111	1 skein
Terracotta	883	1 skein
Yellow	292	1 skein
Leaf Green	253	2 skeins
Mid Green	266	2 skeins
Dark Green	268	2 skeins
Pale Blue	159	1 skein
Mid Blue	161	1 skein

White interlocked canvas, 14 holes to the inch.
Canvas size: 10in × 10in (26 × 26cm)
Size 20 needle
Ruler or tape measure
Masking tape for binding the canvas
Sharp scissors for cutting the canvas
Embroidery scissors
Sharp HB pencil or fine permanent marker in a suitable colour
Eraser

HOW TO MARK THE CANVAS
Cut the canvas to size and tape the edges. Trace the design (page 185) onto the centre of the canvas using a permanent marker or HB pencil. It is only necessary to trace the thick lines. The thin lines denote a change of colour and can be drawn on freehand afterwards. Alternatively, trace the fine

lines onto the canvas in another colour. Ignore the dotted lines; they are the guide lines for the stems and are to be stitched after the design has been appliquéd onto the cushion.

HOW TO STITCH
Use six strands (the whole thread) throughout.

Stitches used
1 tent stitch
2 split back stitch
3 satin stitch
4 long and short stitch
5 French knots

The stitch cards will show you how to do the stitches. The numbers on the colour drawing refer to the numbers on the stitch cards. Refer to the colour drawing to show you which colours go where. The arrows show you the direction of the stitches.

The violets are sewn in LONG AND SHORT stitch (4) radiating out from the centres. The centres are FRENCH KNOTS (5); the stems of the flowers and the veins of the leaves are in SPLIT BACK stitch (2). The leaves are worked in TENT stitch (1). The ribbon has been stitched in diagonal SATIN stitch (3).

MAKING UP INSTRUCTIONS
When the design has been stitched it may be necessary to stretch it back into shape (Chapter 15), then appliqué it onto a suitable cushion or chair-back (again, Chapter 15).

After you have stitched the appliqué into place, sew the stems onto the fabric in the appropriate colour stranded cotton in BACK stitch, following the dotted lines on the tracing. Use the whole thread (6 strands) and use fairly big stitches.

We have appliquéd the design onto a white lace cushion and love the delicacy of this look. You may have an existing cushion on which the violets would look equally good.

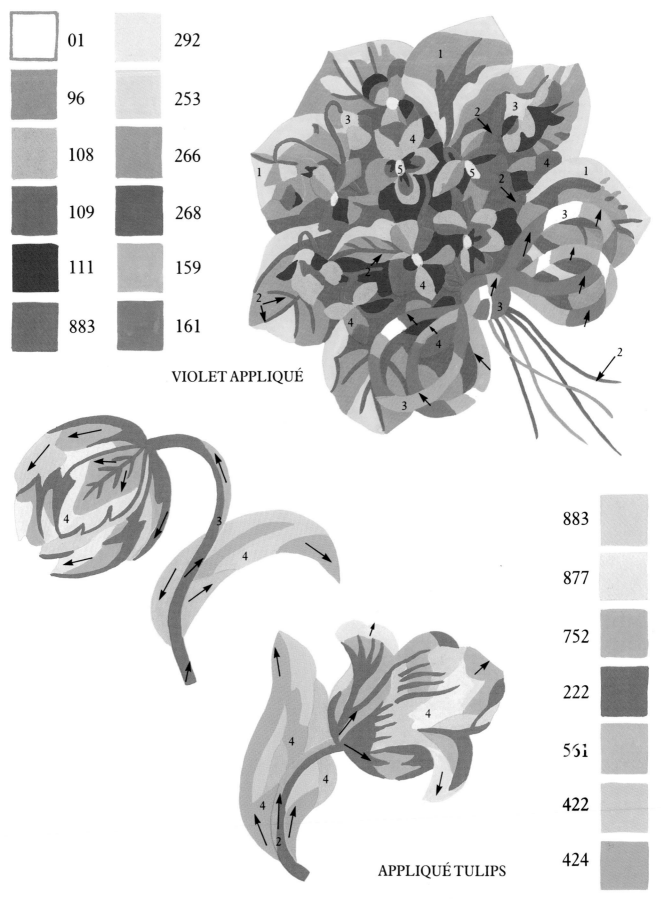

01

96

108

109

111

883

292

253

266

268

159

161

VIOLET APPLIQUÉ

883

877

752

222

561

422

424

APPLIQUÉ TULIPS

APPLIQUÉ TULIPS

Finished size of design: 5 to 6in (13 to 15cm)
Tracings: pages 186/7

MATERIALS
Appleton's tapestry wool

Heather   883 ⅛ hank (9 × 30in/75cm lengths)
Pale Peach   877 ⅛ hank (9 × 30in/75cm lengths)
Pink   752 ⅛ hank (9 × 30in/75cm lengths)
Terracotta   222 ¼ hank (18 × 30in/75cm lengths)
Blue   561 ⅛ hank (9 × 30in/75cm lengths)
Apple Green 422 ⅛ hank (9 × 30in/75cm lengths)
Leaf Green   424 ⅛ hank (9 × 30in/75cm lengths)

White interlocked canvas, 14 holes to the inch
Canvas size: 12in × 9in (31 × 23cm)
Size 20 needle
Ruler or tape measure
Masking tape for binding the canvas
Sharp scissors for cutting the canvas
Embroidery scissors
Sharp HB pencil or fine permanent marker in a suitable
  colour, and eraser

HOW TO MARK THE CANVAS
Cut the canvas to size and tape the edges.

Trace the tulips (pages 186/7) onto the canvas keeping them at least 1in (2.5cm) apart. Trace the thick lines and put the thin lines in afterwards, either freehand or by tracing. The thin lines are to show the change in the shade of wool.

HOW TO STITCH
Use the whole thread throughout.

Stitches used
2 split back stitch
3 satin stitch
4 long and short stitch

The stitch cards will show you how to do the stitches. The numbers on the coloured drawing refer to the numbers on the stitch cards. Refer to the colour picture and the drawing to show you which colour goes where. The arrows show the direction of the stitches.

The tulips are worked in LONG AND SHORT stitch (4); stems in SPLIT BACK (2) and SATIN stitch (3).

You can do as many or as few of the appliqués as you wish, and you could also sew the background and make the design into a stool, a cushion or a chairseat.

MAKING UP INSTRUCTIONS
After the designs have been sewn, it may be necessary to refer to Chapter 15 for instructions on how to stretch them back into shape and then appliqué, or for how to make up into cushions.

Right Tulip Appliqué –
shown on the Tulip chair

CHAPTER 13
RUGS

The image of the tree has appeared in the art and dreams of man as an image of mystery and power, from archaic mythology to the twentieth century. It represents his desire to grasp the essential reality of the world; it links earth and heaven, rooted in darkness, expanding into light. We have used many trees in many forms, in styles from Islamic to Naive, yet the 'Tree of Life Rug' is the simplest and most suggestive of the rich symbolism this subject attracts. The design moves out from the central point, flowing in all directions, and needs a larger expanse than a cushion or a picture. This was our first needlepoint rug and since then we have produced many, in many styles, but this one is still very special to us.

Needlepoint rugs are very beautiful—there is a flatness and richness to them which we love, and the cross stitches give a satisfyingly solid texture. We felt that it was time for a rug revival—the Victorians loved needlepoint rugs but later they dwindled in popularity. We have become an impatient society and not too many people look for long projects. The individual rugs and carpets we had produced over the years had pleased us very much and we couldn't believe that the customers who had commissioned them were so rare a breed. So, with the Tree of Life image looking for a surface on which to live, we began our first mass-produced rug. We were overwhelmed by the response.

The depressed Yorkshire mill which we first visited to see precisely how the Tree of Life would be stencilled (by hand, as it turned out, in pre-industrial era style) returned to life, and we were delighted that we had initiated the revival of interest. We use 5-hole canvas, which is so encouragingly fast to work that the rug grows with visible speed. However enjoyable a project is, you don't want to be doing it forever. The wool we use is 4-ply and dyed for us in 'Glorafilia' shades. There is a flow to working a cross stitch rug which is different from the hooked method, and makes it very relaxing to do. A rug can be done as a group project (therapy or otherwise!). Give your friends a needle, show them the direction of the crossover of the stitch so that all stitches look uniform, stand back and watch them become absorbed.

Seven-hole canvas doesn't sound much smaller than 5-hole, but it is in fact almost twice the number of holes—forty-nine stitches to the square inch as opposed to twenty-five, and we use this when we want to achieve more definition in the design. We have also designed rugs on 10-canvas, which is twice as fine again (100 stitches to the square inch) and allows for even finer detail. However, in general—because a rug is large and seen on the floor and not in close up (and we have had no criticism of our designs from cats)—we feel 7-hole canvas gives sufficiently fine detail for even an intricate design.

A rug is less daunting than might be imagined. For the mathematically minded there are in fact less stitches on a 5-holes-to-the-inch rug than on a 14-holes-to-the-inch cushion.

The rug we have charted is the Tulip Rug, which has the look of a dhurrie and has been one of our most popular designs. We work all our rugs in cross stitch to give strength; the thickness of wool back and front and the canvas make them extremely hardwearing. We once estimated that 20,000 people walked over the Ribbon Rug during an exhibition—we had it dry cleaned and the rug is as perfect as the day it was finished. Unless you have an unusual social life, this is more traffic than an average rug would receive in front of an average fireplace.

Some people use a floor frame for working rugs, but it isn't essential. You can work a rug wherever is most comfortable for you. Start it on your lap and, as it becomes heavier, put it on a table, where it will be supported by its own weight. Work on the part between the table edge and your lap, one hand behind, one in front, passing the needle back and forth, as if working on a frame.

Overleaf Rugs! The Tree of Life is draped over the back of the stone bench

Right The Ribbon Rug and matching cushions

144

TULIP RUG

Finished size of design:
   without fringing: 32in × 43in (81 × 109cm)
   with fringing: 32in × 53in (81 × 135cm)

MATERIALS
Glorafilia 4 ply rug wool in BALLS

Cream	(Shade ref G)	9 balls
Pale Peach	(Shade ref J)	9 balls
Mint Green	(Shade ref I)	6 balls
Leaf Green	(Shade ref L)	4 balls
Oyster Pink	(Shade ref K)	4 balls
Stone	(Shade ref H)	4 balls

1⅓m (52in) cream rug canvas 36in (90cm) wide, 5 holes to the inch
Size 13 needle
Masking tape for binding the canvas
Sharp scissors for cutting the canvas
Embroidery scissors and tape measure/ruler

THE CANVAS
The canvas does not have to be marked out, just follow the colour chart. See General Information for useful hints on working from a colour chart.

HOW TO STITCH
The whole thread is used throughout, in cross stitch (25).

Cut the canvas to size and bind the edges. The stitch card will show you how to do the stitch.

Cut your thread approximately 30in (75cm) in length. The rug is sewn in CROSS stitch (25) throughout which makes it hard wearing and gives a textured look. We suggest you begin stitching at the top right hand corner and work horizontally filling in blocks of colour. It is not necessary to use a frame, but the rug will be easier to handle should you decide to use one. You will need a 36in (or larger) floor standing frame (see General Information). If you do not use a frame the following method can be used: place the rug on a table and put weights on top to stop it moving; sit at the table and begin stitching, moving the position of the rug according to the area you are sewing.

If you decide to stitch curled up in a chair, make sure you support the weight of the sewn areas.

MAKING UP INSTRUCTIONS
Stretch the rug back into shape and make up into a rug. For fringing and backing see Chapter 15.

TULIP
RUG

J

K

H

I

L

G

CHAPTER 14
SAMPLERS

Samuel Johnson's eighteenth-century definition of the word sampler was 'a piece worked by young girls for improvement'. Samplers, which are so prized today, were often done by children at a very young age, as something vital to learn, as part of a way of life. These samplers are charming and sad, with their often morbid verses. Imagine how many hours must have been spent and tears shed—'sad sewers sew sad samplers'—and compare them to the samplers of today which are worked to celebrate an occasion.

The word sampler, originating from the Latin, has come down to us from the French 'exemplaire' and become anglicised to saumpler, sampler or exampler. The samplers were either a beginner's specimen of her skill, or a collection of techniques and patterns put together as a reference—books on the subject were not yet in existence. A sampler was, literally, an example, similar to a scrap book. The child would keep these references for later life, either when she went into service, or as a lady with her own servants, overseeing the maintenance of clothing and household linen. Until the twentieth century much of a poor girl's early education was needlework, considered more important than reading or writing, as a functional necessity and not for recreational pleasure. The upper classes used sewing as a leisurely accomplishment, but the less

privileged girl often went into service where needlework skills were essential for darning and marking linens. Hence, darning samplers came about—several patches in different styles of darning to clearly show as a reference, particularly for use on damask cloths. In the mid-eighteenth century quite a large repertoire of stitches was used on samplers. By the end of the century, only cross stitch remained.

For the sampler project shown opposite, we have reverted to a variety of stitches. Various sources have been used as the inspiration for this picture, which we designed as a wedding sampler. The majority of the motifs were adapted from a piece worked by Hannah Taylor in America in 1774—some were influenced by American crewel work. You can, of course, alter the centre and make more room for lettering if you prefer. Or add more motifs in a random way, which is quite often seen on older samplers.

We have designed several samplers 'in the traditional style'. Among those we particularly like is the Sophie and William sampler shown overleaf, which is typical of mid-nineteenth-century samplers intended to be purely decorative needlework pictures; and the one with the deer, where the background is left unworked to imitate the linen samplers.

| *Right* Colonial sampler

Some nineteenth-century and twentieth-century samplers. The experimental strip of fabric illustrates well the 'scrap book', or reference, function of early samplers

THE BAINBRIDGE SAMPLER

This unique sampler, with its unusual design of geometric shapes, was drawn by an unknown hand 130 years ago. The individual panels are finely embroidered, each by a different person named on the little plan shown. Those involved—men and women—have been traced by Nan Bainbridge, the owner of the tapestry, and her cousin, both granddaughters of A. E. Elsey, who is named on the plan and who completed the unfinished sampler. It then travelled to America and on to Australia, where it was found by Nan while she was going through old papers. Most of the people mentioned on the plan came from Horncastle in Lincolnshire, and included a stonemason, a cornmiller, a wool draper and an auctioneer. The anonymous needle-workers of this beautiful piece became real—but what was the motivation for these hat makers and bird-stuffers to begin such a piece of work? And would people do this today?

These last questions are the reason why this sampler is such a delight to us. It is not only beautiful, but is full of an exuberance often lacking in antique needlework. Just to look at this heirloom makes us itch to begin something similar ourselves, involving family and friends. The Bainbridge Sampler is elegantly conceived, with overall balance and strong harmony, and one clearly hears the voice of an overseer organising. What would have been far more telling is the *individual* choice of each participant—the result couldn't possibly be as attractive, but in terms of nostalgia . . .

Ideally, each person should design his own section and the director general organise the use of the yarns to achieve consistency. Each section could have discreet initials of its designer and stitcher. For your own family sampler there will be many motifs from which to choose—the family house; a favourite pet; interests such as music, books, astrological signs; interwoven initials and dates; a remembered wedding bouquet, a baby's first shoes . . . once you begin, you will think of dozens of ideas.

COLONIAL SAMPLER

Finished size of design: 10½in × 12½in (27 × 32cm)
Tracings: pages 188/9

MATERIALS
Appleton's crewel wool
White	991	2 skeins
Peach	705	1 skein
Terracotta	205	2 skeins
Pale Mauve	711	1 skein
Dark Mauve	713	2 skeins
Blue	876	1 skein
Turquoise	562	1 skein
Custard	851	2 skeins
Leaf Green	353	2 skeins
Green	151	1 skein
Peacock Green	642	4 skeins
Bright Gold	474	2 skeins
Ginger	475	2 skeins

Anchor stranded cotton
Ecru	387	10 skeins

Interlocked white canvas, 18 holes to the inch
Size of canvas: 14in × 16in (36 × 41cm)
Size 22 needle
Small piece of tracing paper
Ruler or tape measure
Masking tape for binding the canvas
Sharp scissors for cutting the canvas
Embroidery scissors
Sharp HB pencil or fine permanent marker in a suitable colour
Eraser

HOW TO MARK THE CANVAS
Cut the canvas to size and tape the edges. Mark out the canvas using an HB pencil or permanent marker in a pale shade. The graph has been drawn to scale. Each square of the graph represents one hole of the canvas and the lines represent the threads. Count the squares and then draw the outline of the border and the central dividing lines all on the thread of the canvas.

Trace the motifs (pages 188/9) onto the border and then onto the middle, taking care to position them correctly as the canvas is not always absolutely 'square'. Use the colour picture (page 153) and the colour drawing as your guide. The thick lines are the outline of the motifs, the fine lines show a change of colour. If you are confident, copy the fine lines freehand in another colour. Otherwise these can be traced on afterwards.

Decide on the script initials you want and trace these from page 169 centring them in the middle of the heart. Then trace the numbers and letters you require from pages 172/3 onto a piece of tracing paper before tracing them onto the canvas. It is easier to transfer the numbers/letters if you plan the words first. If the date is too long, use a short form ie JAN instead of January, or numbers, ie 4.5.89. You can use more of the centre for personalising if you wish by leaving out some of the flowers.

HOW TO STITCH
Two strands of crewel wool have been used throughout with the exception of the background when six strands of stranded cotton (the whole thread) have been used.

Stitches used
1 tent stitch
2 split back stitch
3 satin stitch
4 long and short stitch
5 French knots
12 upright cross stitch
17 continuous mosaic stitch
19 chain stitch

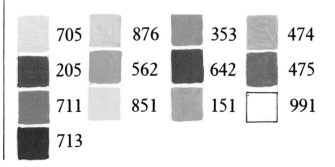

705 876 353 474
205 562 642 475
711 851 151 991
713

The stitch cards will show you how to do the stitches. The numbers on the coloured drawing refer to the numbers on the stitch cards. Refer to the colour picture and drawing to show you which colour goes where and the direction of the stitches.

Before stitching please read the following. *Unless otherwise marked* all stems, veins and outlining are in SPLIT BACK stitch (2); leaves are in SATIN stitch (3). Letters and numbers are in SPLIT BACK stitch (2). The background and the green dividing lines are in TENT stitch (1). The gold borders are in diagonal SATIN stitch (3) worked over two rows in gold and ginger—see diagonal lines for direction. The direction changes in the middle of each line—see dotted lines on the coloured artwork and Diagram 1.

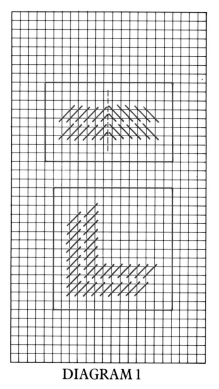

DIAGRAM 1

The areas to be sewn in white on the flowers have been clearly outlined, to separate them from the background which is worked in ecru cotton.

Leave the ecru background until the end—the cotton will lose its sheen if handled excessively. Ensure that you have no strands of wool loose at the back, as they may become caught up with the cotton.

Begin by sewing the central area, the letters and numbers followed by the motifs. The butterflies are in diagonal SATIN stitch (3) and the ladybird is also in diagonal SATIN stitch (3) and TENT stitch (1). The flowers are worked in SATIN stitch (3) radiating out from the centre and the flower centres are in TENT stich (1). The vase is in diagonal SATIN stitch (3). Work the green dividing lines and the inside border.

The flowers on the border are worked in LONG AND SHORT stitch (4) and SATIN stitch (3) radiating out from the centre with some flower centres in TENT stitch (1). The urns are worked in UPRIGHT CROSS stitch (12). Sew the leaves and stems and then the strawberries in TENT stitch (1). Work the script initials in the middle of the heart which has been sewn in CHAIN stitch (19) filled in with TENT stitch (1). The man and the woman are in TENT stitch (1), hair and hat in diagonal SATIN stitch (3). The bench is in SATIN stitch (3) also. The mauve flowers are in FRENCH KNOTS (5). Work the trees in CONTINUOUS MOSAIC stitch (17), tree trunks in diagonal SATIN stitch (3). The bird is in diagonal SATIN stitch (3).

Finally, sew the outside border and then the background in ecru stranded cotton.

MAKING UP INSTRUCTIONS
When you have finished sewing, the design may need to be stretched back into shape (see Chapter 15). You may prefer to take your tapestry to a professional picture framer who will also stretch it for you.

CHAPTER 15
FINISHING AND MAKING UP

STRETCHING

MATERIALS
Blotting paper
A flat clean board
Tacks
Staples or drawing pins

The needlepoint must be 'square' before framing or making into a cushion, stool, rug, etc. If out of square the tapestry should be lightly damped or sprayed and left for a few minutes to soften the canvas. Gently pull square and then pin out, right side down, onto blotting paper on a flat, clean board. Use tacks, staples or drawing pins and pin outside the sewn surface. Do not strain too tightly or the tapestry will dry with a scalloped edge. When *thoroughly dry*, remove from the board. This may take two to three days.

MAKING THE NEEDLEPOINT INTO A SET-IN CUSHION WITH MITRED CORNERS.

MATERIALS
½ metre (20in) fabric 48in wide (velvet is very difficult to work with if you are not experienced)
A zip 3in (7.5cm) smaller than the *finished* cushion size
Piping cord (No 3)
1 Cushion pad 2in (5cm) *larger* than the *finished* cushion
Pins

1   When cutting the back of the cushion add 4in (10cm) to the size of the tapestry from top to bottom and 6in (15cm) from side to side. This allows for the border around the tapestry. A ½in (1.25cm) turning has been allowed for all seams except for each side of the zip for which we have allowed 1in (2.5cm) (see cutting plan).

2   Cut out the back and fold in half lengthwise, cut along the crease—this is for the zip opening.
3   Cut four borders 2½in × 6in (6.25 × 15cm) longer than the size of the tapestry (see cutting plan).
4   Cut piping 1½in (4cm) wide on the cross at a 45 degree angle. Place the two back pieces right sides together and taking a 1in (2.5cm) turning sew down 1½in (4cm). Repeat this at the other end. Sew in zip taking a 1in (2.5cm) turning on each side.

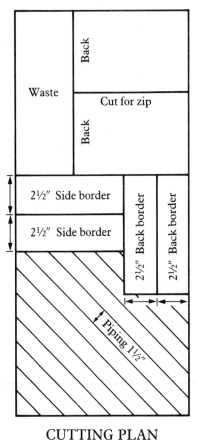

CUTTING PLAN

5   Sew piping strips together (Fig A). Press seams open and trim off projecting points (Fig B).

6   Fit borders by laying the front border onto the front of the tapestry overlapping ½in (1.25cm) onto the finished tapestry (Fig C). Pin to the edge of the tapestry. Fold back the material to form a mitre and press a crease. Do this to all the borders. Tack mitres and then machine them together. Trim away the excess material eaving a ½in (1.25cm) seam.

7   To attach the piping to the border, fold the piping strip right side outermost and lengthwise. Insert piping cord into the fold and tack into place on the right side of the border, allowing ½in (1.25cm) turning. Clip piping strip at corners and leave strip open for several inches at the end, for the final joining of the piping. Place one open end behind the other and mark with pins at the point where the two ends overlap by ½in (1.25cm). Cut underneath strip at diagonal angle (Fig D) and machine together. Butt the two ends of cord into each other and insert back into the strip. Machine with half foot keeping close to cord. Do this to both edges (Fig E).

8   Tack the piped border to the edge of the tapestry right sides together, clipping corners, machine and then trim off the excess canvas leaving a ½in (1.25cm) of the cushion seam.

9   Tack the back of the cushion to the front, machine and then double stitch or overlock the seams.

MAKING THE NEEDLEPOINT INTO A SQUARE BOXED CUSHION

MATERIALS
½ metre (20in) of fabric 48in wide (velvet is very difficult to work with if you are not experienced)
A zip 3in (7.5cm) smaller than the *finished* cushion size
1 Boxed cushion pad 2in (5cm) *larger* than the *finished* cushion
Piping cord (No 3)
Pins

1   Cut out the fabric backing of the cushion the same size as the tapestry including unsewn edge from top to bottom, and 2in (5cm) wider from side to side. Fold in half lengthwise and cut down the crease—this is to form the zip opening.

2   Cut two borders 3in (7.5cm) by the width of your cushion and another two, 3in (7.5cm) by the length of your cushion.

3   Cut the piping 1½in (3.75cm) wide on the cross at a 45 degree angle.

4   To size the borders take the back border and lay it right side to right side of the tapestry. Cut any excess fabric protruding over the canvas (Fig F). Do this to the sides and the front border. Pin or tack back border to the side borders and the front to the sides.

5   Notch the front of the cushion and front border. Machine the seams together and pipe the border and both sides taking ½in (1.25cm) turning. Following the instructions for a mitred cushion, tack the front border, right sides together to the front of the cushion matching the notches, clipping the border seams to turn the corners (Fig G). Sew the zip in the back of the cushion taking 1in (2.5cm) turning either side of the zip. Tack the back to the cushion. Machine and then double stitch or overlock the seams.

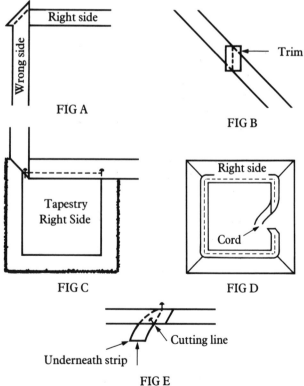

FIG A

FIG B

FIG C

FIG D

FIG E

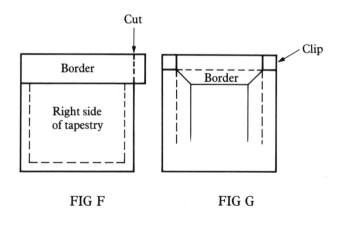

FIG F

FIG G

MAKING THE NEEDLEPOINT INTO A ROUND BOXED CUSHION

MATERIALS

½ metre (20in) fabric 48in wide (velvet is very difficult to work with if you are not experienced)
A zip 3in (7.5cm) *smaller* than the *finished* cushion size
Piping cord (No 3)
1 Round boxed cushion pad 2in (5cm) *larger* than the *finished* cushion
Pins

1 Cut away the excess canvas leaving ½in (1.25cm) of unsewn canvas for turning. Cut the fabric depending on the size of the cushion, if a large round tapestry you will need to cut two strips 3in × 48in (7.5 × 120cm) for borders.
2 Cut the back of the cushion the same size as the overall tapestry from top to bottom and 2in (5cm) wider from side to side.
3 Cut the piping 1½in (3.75cm) wide on the cross at a 45 degree angle. Fold the backing in half lengthwise and cut down the crease—this is to form the zip opening. Place the two back pieces right sides together and taking a 1in (2.5cm) turning sew down 1½in (3.75cm). Repeat this at the other end. Sew in the zip taking 1in (2.5cm) turning on each side.
4 Using the tapestry, including the unsewn edge, as a pattern, place the right side of the tapestry to the right side of the backing. Pin into place and cut the backing the same size as the tapestry.
5 If you are using two borders, join them together at one end. Place the border right side to right side of the tapestry. Pin the border around the tapestry very carefully, clipping the edges as you go (see Fig H). When you have gone all round the tapestry, overlap the open end of the border 1in (2.5cm) and cut away the excess to allow a ½in (1.25cm) turning. Stitch this seam to close the open ends of the border. Unpin the border from the tapestry and

pipe the border following the instructions for the mitred cushion. Tack the piped border to the edge of the tapestry right sides together and then machine. Tack back to the other side of the border and machine, and then double stitch or overlock the seams.

MAKING UP THE NEEDLEPOINT INTO A SPECTACLE CASE

MATERIALS

Three pieces of fabric 8½ in × 5in (22 × 13cm) in an appropriate colour

After stretching the design back into shape, trim the canvas leaving a ½in (1.25cm) border of unsewn canvas on the sides and bottom. Cut out the backing the same size as the canvas, and cut another two pieces the same size for lining. With right sides of spectacle case together, machine or back stitch as close to the design as possible leaving the top open. Turn back to the right side and hem down the top of the canvas and the backing. Machine the lining right sides together taking a good ½in (1.5cm) turning. Put the lining inside the spectacle case, turn down the top of the lining and hem to the top of the spectacle case.

MAKING UP THE NEEDLEPOINT INTO A BOOKMARK

MATERIALS

A piece of fabric 10in × 3in (26 × 8cm)

After stretching the design back into shape, trim the unsewn canvas leaving ½in (1.25cm) for turning.
Cut out in the same way as the spectacle case. Place right side of fabric to the right side of the tapestry. Tack together leaving the top open. Machine or back stitch close to the finished work. Then cut straight across the corners leaving ¼in (.5cm) so that it will lay flat. Turn back to the right side and neaten the top.

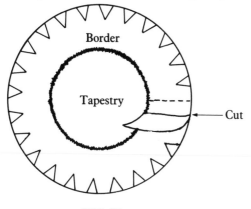

FIG H

MAKING UP THE NEEDLEPOINT INTO A PHOTO-FRAME

MATERIALS
Thick celluloid for the front 4in × 6in (11 × 15cm)
A felt tip marker in a matching colour
Bulldog clips
Hardboard panel 6¾in × 8in (17.5cm × 20cm)
Photo-frame strut back in the same size as the hardboard
  panel (obtainable from a frame maker)
Copydex or similar
Coloured paper or fabric in a suitable colour
Thin sponge

This is not an easy project to enter into. We do suggest that you take the sewn photograph frame to a framer for a professional finish. However, if you are adventurous and have lots of patience, go ahead.

Stretch the canvas back into shape. Using a felt tip marker of a matching colour, stain the canvas to a width of about ½in (1.25cm) from all wool edges. This prevents white edges showing on the finished job.

1   Mark out and cut an ⅛in (3mm) wide hardboard panel ⅛in (3mm) smaller all round than the sewn tapestry, with a square opening ⅛in (3mm) larger all round than the tapestry centre. Bevel the inside and outside edges. Using a suitable adhesive (Copydex) cover the face of the panel with ⅜in (1cm) wide foam sponge. Bevel the edges with a sharp knife.

2   Before stretching, trim the canvas to about 1in (2.5cm) all round and cut the corners as in the diagram. Stretch over the panel using Copydex or similar. Glue the back of the panel and fold the canvas round. Do not glue any part of the wool. Start with two opposite sides, then the other two sides. Work the wool edge to the panel edge and use bulldog clips to hold the canvas in position until set. With a sharp knife or scissors cut the unsewn canvas in the centre as shown on the diagram. Glue the canvas onto the hardboard using the same procedure as before. Trim the excess canvas.

3   Obtain a photo-frame strut back the same size as the hardboard panel. (can be obtained from a frame maker). Cut and glue on 2in (5cm) strips of ⅛in (3mm) hardboard or cardboard at the top and two side edges. Bind the raw edges of the strut back with a suitable colour tape (cloth, paper or plastic). For a professional finish cover the whole back and edges including the strut leg with coloured paper. Cut a piece of thick celluloid or similar to fit the recess created.

4   Finally, glue the tapestry bound panel and the strut back together with Copydex. Use bulldog clips until completely set. Slide photograph and celluloid in slot at bottom. To prevent picture from slipping down in the frame, tape into position on the plastic.

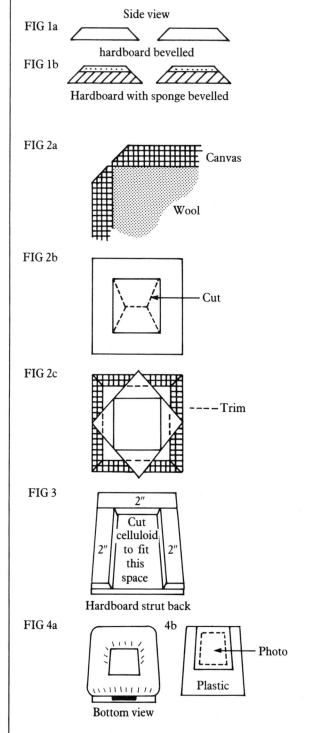

FIG 1a   Side view
hardboard bevelled

FIG 1b
Hardboard with sponge bevelled

FIG 2a   Canvas
Wool

FIG 2b   Cut

FIG 2c   ---- Trim

FIG 3
2"
Cut celluloid to fit this space
2"   2"
Hardboard strut back

FIG 4a   4b   Photo
Plastic
Bottom view

MAKING UP THE NEEDLEPOINT INTO A ROUND PICTURE

MATERIALS
A 7½in (19cm) diameter frame. (can be obtained from Glorafilia)
Thin sponge if desired
Copydex or similar

Cut the tapestry leaving a border of 1in (2.5cm) unsewn canvas. A better look is achieved if the picture is padded with very thin sponge, but this is not essential. Glue the tapestry over the cardboard disc provided, with Copydex or similar—only the unsewn canvas should be glued. Place frame face down and insert mounted tapestry. Insert hardboard backing disc over the mounted tapestry, smooth side showing, and check that the mounting hole corresponds with the top of the tapestry. Turn the three brass buttons to hold the framed tapestry together—this should be a snug fit.

MAKING UP THE NEEDLEPOINT INTO A ROUND STOOL

MATERIALS
1 stool 10in diameter (25cm) (can be obtained from Glorafilia)
⅜in tacks
Strong thread

After the design has been stretched back into shape, thread a tapestry needle with a length of strong thread and work running stitches around the canvas about ¾in (2cm) on the outside of the sewn circle, to form a draw string. Place the tapestry face down on the table and centre the padded top onto the tapestry with plywood upwards. Ask someone to place their hand in the centre of the plywood and press downwards, then pull both ends of the drawstring, thus pulling the tapestry edges over the plywood base; tie firmly with a bow. With a little patience and perseverance at this stage it is possible to ease out the gathers and obtain a very even finish around the edge. Leave the top for one or two days to allow the canvas to stretch, then make final adjustments easing out gathers again if necessary. Now tack to the underside of the plywood base with ⅜in tacks, ½in (1.25cm) from the edge and ½in to ¾in (1.25 to 2cm) apart. Trim off surplus canvas with scissors or a craft knife ¾in (2cm) from the edge. Place the padded top into the stool base, turn upside down and twist the wood screw.

MAKING THE NEEDLEPOINT INTO A PIN-CUSHION

MATERIALS
A piece of fabric in an appropriate colour 1in (2.5cm) larger than the sewn pincushion—6½in × 6½in (17cm)
Pins
Stuffing—kapok or Terylene filling
Pot-pourri (if desired)
Tassels

After stretching back into shape, cut the excess unsewn canvas, leaving a ½in (1.25cm) border all round. With right sides together, tack the backing material to the unsewn canvas, sewing as close to the design as possible. Then machine or back stitch leaving an opening of approximately 2 to 3in (5 to 7.5cm). Turn back to the right side.

Stuff the pincushion as full as possible using kapok or Terylene filling, mixed with pot-pourri. Finally, close the opening, using slip stitch.

MAKING THE TASSELS
Cut twelve strands of left-over yarn approximately 30in (75cm) long for each tassel. Fold in half and half again. Take a strand of yarn and wrap round centre two or three times. With the excess strand of yarn make a loop. Then make three crochet chains from the loop, but leave the length of wool intact to sew on the finished pincushion. Fold at the chain and with another strand of yarn wrap around ½in (1.25cm) down from the top of the tassel. Finish off securely. Cut through the loops at the bottom of the tassel. Finally sew onto the pincushion.

MAKING UP THE SILVER TABBY CAT

MATERIALS
Grey or black felt 12in × 16in (31 × 41cm)
Kapok or Terylene filling
Tracing paper
Pins

After the design has been stretched back into shape, cut out leaving ½in (1.25cm) for turnings. .Place this onto the felt, sewn side down and pin into place. Cut out the felt to the shape of the design (including the ½in (1.25cm) unsewn canvas). Take a tracing of the pattern for the base and then cut a piece of felt to the same shape. Tack one half of the bottom of the design onto the base. Tack the design to the felt backing, leaving the other half of the base open and sew into place. Clip all inward shapes of canvas so that it will lay flat when turned to the right side. Turn to the right side and stuff with kapok or Terylene. Close the opening using slip stitch.

MAKING UP THE NEEDLEPOINT INTO A DOORSTOP

MATERIALS
A brick approximately 8½in × 4in × 2in (22 × 10.5 × 6.5cm) (British Standard Brick size) available from the builders merchants
A piece of felt or canvas for the base, approximately 12in × 6½in (30 × 16cm)
Pins

After stretching the needlepoint back into shape cut out the canvas leaving ¾in (1.5cm) for turning. Pin A to B right sides together to form the shape then machine or back stitch on the underside, taking care that no unworked canvas shows on the right side. Trim the canvas at the corners. Turn to the right side and then insert the brick. Fold the unsewn excess canvas over the brick and stitch at the corners. Pin fabric base onto the underside of the doorstop, turning as you go along and sew into position.

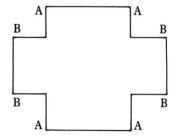

SILVER TABBY CAT
BASE
ACTUAL SIZE

MAKING UP THE NEEDLEPOINT INTO AN APPLIQUÉ

Appliqué designs are extremely versatile. They can either be appliquéd onto an existing cushion, purchased separately and the finished shape is up to you—circular, square, heart shaped—ideal for cushions, pictures, chair seats or chair backs.

MATERIALS

A finished cushion, or chair back etc
Suitable thread—crewel wool or stranded cotton in the same colours as the appliqué is sewn in
Pins

After stretching the canvas back into shape, cut out the design leaving ½in (1.25cm) border all the way round. Turn in the ½in (1.25cm) border and press down. Pin or tack the appliqué onto the fabric right side up, keeping it as flat as possible. Thread a pointed needle with one strand of crewel wool or two or three strands of embroidery cotton in a shade that will complement the design. Change the colour where the colour changes on the appliqué. Turning in as you go along, stitch the design onto the fabric using hem stitch. Use small stitches close together.

FRINGING AND MAKING UP THE RUG

MATERIALS

3 balls of fringing wool*
1 latchet*
Rug backing, 1in (2.5cm) bigger than the size of the rug*
  *can be obtained from Glorafilia

FRINGING THE RUG

1   Fold the canvas at the edge of the sewn work.
2   The fringing yarn should be cut into lengths of 12in (30cm).
3   Using the latchet hook, knot two 12in (30cm) lengths into each hole of the last row of the completed rug, working left to right as follows: hold the latchet hook in your right hand and push it up through the canvas. The ends of the fringing wool should be held in the left hand, doubled over to form a loop, with the loop hanging down. Hook the two loops under the hook and pull the loop through the canvas 3in (7.5cm). Unhook the latchet and feed the four ends through the loop pulling tightly into a knot, which will form a tassel.
4   When the row is finished tie the tassels in the following order:
Starting from the left, take the first and third tassels, tie them together using an overhand knot—see diagram and tighten the knot about 1in (2.5cm) from the end of the rug. Next take the second and fifth, and knot these together in the same way. Continue in this way, knotting the fourth and seventh, the sixth and ninth tassels, and so on until the row has been completed.
5   Trim away uneven ends with a pair of scissors and repeat at the other end of the rug.

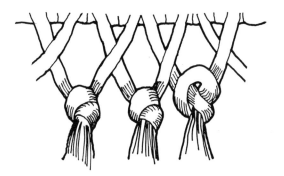

MAKING UP AND BACKING THE RUG

Lay the rug face downwards on a table, turn back the selvedges and stitch down. Lay the backing over the rug, smooth out and turn under the surplus of about ½in (1.25cm) all round and stitch the edges of the backing to the edges of the rug. It is advisable to run a row of stitches across the width of the backing at about 1in (2.5cm) from each end of the backing. This will prevent it from bunching. Use the foam side for uncarpeted areas and the hessian side for carpeted areas.

SCRIPT INITIALS LETTERS AND NUMBERS

To trace the initial, numbers and letters onto the canvas, simply place the canvas over the initial you require and trace using an HB pencil or permanent marker in a suitable colour (see pages 169, 172/3, 186/7).

TRACINGS, ALPHABETS
AND
NUMBERS

CHECKERBOARD
GARDENIA

A B C D E F
G H I J K L M
N O P Q R S T
U V W X Y Z

BUTTERFLY
TRELLIS

JERUSALEM

A B C D E F G H I J K L M N
O P Q R S T U V W X Y Z

COPELAND SPODE FRUIT PLATE

1234567890

COPELAND SPODE FLOWER PLATE

TREE POPPIES

INTERWOVEN
RIBBONS

FAN

TOP
RIGHT

TOP
LEFT

PEONY

BOTTOM
RIGHT

BOTTOM
LEFT

BUTTERFLY

FRUIT
PINCUSHION

MING PARROTS

CLUNY
SPECTACLE CASE

CLUNY
BOOKMARK

MISTY
ANEMONES

181

JAPANESE IRISES AND BUTTERFLIES

MONET'S POPPIES

VIOLET APPLIQUÉ

APPLIQUÉ TULIPS

186

COLONIAL SAMPLER

ACKNOWLEDGEMENTS

We are delighted to have this opportunity to thank everyone who has been involved with us in this book.

To David Jordan, for his beautiful photographs and serene temperament. To all at Glorafilia, particularly Chris Gregory and Daphne King for their multiple skills, Ros Neale and Djien Bishop for their painterly talents, and a special thank you to Shirlee Sharpe for her calming influence and superb efficiency. Thanks to the stitchers, especially Dorothy de Lacy, Andrea Cooper and Geraldine Purdue, who understand the word 'deadline'. To Julie Baldwin, for her consistently perfect cushion-making. And to Janet Peskin, who arrived hopeful and stayed to become an insomniac—a huge thanks for your enthusiastic input.

Thanks to Appleton's—a long-service medal! To Laraine Mortner, Doreen Turner, Evelyn Hope, Johanna Howard, Sue Goldstein, Nan Bainbridge and Pat Schogger. To Ena Green Antiques at Alfies, Church Street, London, to The Gallery of Antique Costume and Textiles, Designers Guild, Liberty and Colefax & Fowler for the loan of fabrics, to *Woman and Home* for the 'Cats' photograph—and enormous thanks to Sally King for tolerating the invasion of her beautiful home. Most important, to our families—the normal high service you have come to expect will now be resumed!

And, of course, to David Green, for reasons he knows best.

INDEX

INDEX